Two Villages
on Stilts

D1286784

CASE STUDIES IN
SOCIAL AND ECONOMIC CHANGE

SERIES EDITORS:

PHILIP H. GULLIVER, Department of Sociology and Anthropology, University of Calgary, Canada

DAVID J. PARKIN, School of Oriental and African Studies, London University

Two Villages on Stilts

Economic and Family Change in Nigeria

STANLEY R. BARRETT

BOWLING GREEN STATE UNIVERSITY
DISCARDED
LIBRARY

CHANDLER PUBLISHING COMPANY
An Intext Publisher
NEW YORK AND LONDON

BOWLING GREEN STATE UNIVERSITY LIBRARY

COPYRIGHT © 1974 BY INTEXT, INC.
All rights reserved. No part of this book may be reprinted,
reproduced, or utilized in any form or by any electronic,
mechanical, or other means, now known or hereafter invented,
including photocopying and recording, or in any information
storage and retrieval system, without permission in writing
from the Publisher.

Library of Congress Cataloging in Publication Data

Barrett, Stanley R.
    Two villages on stilts.

    (Chandler series in social and economic change)
    Bibliography: p.
    1. Villages—Nigeria—Case studies.
2. Collective settlements—Nigeria—Case studies.
3. Family—Nigeria—Case studies. I. Title.
HN800.N5B35   301.42′3′09669   73-19765
ISBN 0-8102-0475-4

Chandler Publishing Co.
257 Park Avenue South
New York, New York 10010

301.4230966
B27+

574366

For
My Parents

571306

CONTENTS

PREFACE

This is a study of the relation between the economy and the family in two Nigerian villages, which I shall call Olowo and Talika. Both villages are located in the stretch of mangrove swamp that separates the Nigerian mainland from the Atlantic Ocean. Because most of this area is flooded during the wet season, houses are built upon stilts. Olowo and Talika are no exception. Hence the title *Two Villages on Stilts*.

This is not a theoretical work in the sense of reporting upon the status of hypotheses that were drawn from established bodies of theory before fieldwork. Such a deductive procedure was hardly possible. This is because neither the significance of the family nor the very existence of Talika were known to me before beginning research. At the same time this study is not devoid of theory. My main concern is to demonstrate the high interdependence of the economic and family institutions, and to entertain the theoretical problems that are generated by the data.

The inductive procedure adopted here is very different from that which I advocated before starting my research. As a student I was impatient with anthropologists who did not choose their project in terms of a problem to be solved, and did not erect models addressed to these problems. In my own case three general models were taken to the field. In a more extensive treatment of Olowo and Talika I hope to show how these models worked. It must suffice for now to say that I no longer look upon general bodies of theory and models as systems of logically interdependent propositions, from which hypotheses can be extrapolated and tested in a rigorous manner. Instead I consider them to be conceptual schemes whose major purpose is to give direction to one's research.

As in the case of theory, I was skeptical of the argument that systematic techniques normally associated with sociology are inapplicable for anthropological research. Again fieldwork experience has forced me to adopt a new position. I now appreciate much more the value of good informants and systematic observation. Nevertheless, I think anthropologists should be more willing to experiment with a wide range of techniques, modifying them to suit the fieldwork case. As well, some indication should be given of the methods used, and especially of the possible biases in the data. Regrettably the limited size of this series allows me only a brief comment.

The main characteristic of my methodology was the combination of anthropological and sociological approaches. In Olowo there was no danger of becoming a complete observer—a role which restricts the kind of questions that can be asked (see Gold, 1958; Junker, 1962)—because it is a tightly-controlled, closed community. As regards informants, I tried to ensure their representativeness, but had difficulty finding reliable candidates among the women (because of my sex) and the high status elderly men. Among my informants there was a strong bias toward young, well-educated male members and hostile nonmembers (both men and women).

Most of my research was conducted in Olowo. Only after the analytic focus sharpened did I move on to Talika. This village is much less of a closed community, and with the exception that no suitable female candidate was found, my informants there were more representative.

A few weeks after fieldwork began, I used a questionnaire to investigate what Olowo people thought about religion. However, it became clear that this tool was not dependable for gathering data on attitudes. Most respondents simply echoed the ideals of the village, rather than revealing what really went on. Shortly after this I began to administer a general questionnaire to the entire population, keeping out all questions concerning attitudes. Although precautions were taken to obtain permission from the village authorities, the questionnaire generated a great deal of hostility among the elderly men and had to be abandoned after three-quarters of the population had been questioned.

Because of this hostility it was necessary to find other techniques to gather systematic data. A successful one was a combination of questionnaire and informant, employing appropriate sampling procedures. From the general questionnaire I had data for 75% of the population. When investigating problems such as residence patterns, I would take a simple random sample from the general questionnaire, compose another questionnaire for the problem at hand (excluding all attitudinal variables), and obtain the services of a reliable informant, who would consider every person selected in the sample in terms of the various questions. Most of the quantitative data for the family in this book were obtained in this way.

Another method that proved useful was what I call a "standing status sample": a sample based on status drawn from the general questionnaire and employed for several projects in which status seemed to be an important variable.[1] Again the procedure was to compose a questionnaire addressed to the problem (such as whether the number of wives of a man varied with status), and then to ask an assistant to consider every case in the sample in terms of the questions. In this book the material for Tables 1 and 2 in the Introduction and 5 and 12 in Chapter 5 was gathered by this method.

Other techniques were used, such as the card-sorting exercise (see Silverman,

---

[1] See note 14 on page 26 for a description of the status sample.

1966) and the structured interview, but the data from them do not appear here. I want to stress that the sociological techniques were not more valuable than the two conventional anthropological ones. Most of my assumptions were generated by participant observation and informants. The questionnaires and other tools were then used to explore them more systematically.

Finally, because most of the people spoke English, I did not attempt to learn the indigenous language, and rarely had to use an interpreter. Even toward the end of fieldwork, my knowledge of Yoruba did not extend much beyond the elaborate greetings, although this was valuable for building rapport.

My greatest debt is to the people of Olowo and Talika who allowed my wife and me to live with them from July 1969 to July 1970. I am especially pleased to pay tribute to the Olowo leader, whose brilliance continually impressed me. I am aware that most of what I write about the village will displease him and his subjects, for they jealously guard their secrets, such as the economic and family changes described in this book. Yet Olowo is a magnificent social experiment, and its story should enrich the knowledge of all who learn about it. I suspect that the leader of the village shares this view, which is why he allowed me to undertake the study.

I owe a debt to Dr. Peter Carstens, Dr. Ralph Beals, and the late Dr. Ian Weinberg (my teachers at the University of Toronto) and to Professor F. G. Bailey and Dr. Peter Lloyd (my teachers at the University of Sussex) for guiding me in theory and fieldwork, respectively. I have also received more healthy criticism from the editors of this series than I could have hoped for.

A generous grant from the Wenner-Gren Foundation made this fieldwork possible, and a doctoral fellowship from the Canada Council supported me while writing up the data for a Ph.D. thesis. Finally, I am indebted to Kaye for typing the manuscript—only one of the many ways in which she contributed to this book.

1. Introduction

Setting

Olowo was founded in 1947 by Yoruba-speaking members of a small religious sect (see McClelland, 1966). With a population in 1970 of over 1200,[1] the village is located along the edge of the Atlantic Ocean in the Niger Delta, separated from the mainland by about 50 miles of swamp. During the wet season most of Ilaje, as the area is called, is covered with water. For this reason not only are houses built upon stilts, but there are no roads, and the main mode of transportation is dug-out canoe. For this reason also there is virtually no modern industry in all of Ilaje.

Olowo has outstanding sociological significance, for in spite of its brief existence and harsh environment, and in contrast to all other Ilaje villages, it has enjoyed rapid economic growth. It has several factories, as well as thriving transport and fishing industries, in which launches and trawlers built in the village are used.

Its standard of living is the envy of other Ilaje villages. In 1953, for example, it became the first settlement in Ilaje to purchase a plant for electricity. Even in 1970 only two other villages in the area enjoyed this amenity. This is not the only innovation that sets Olowo off from the other villages. In the latter villages, people must use canoes to go from one house to another. But Olowo has built a network of boardwalks on stilts that connects all the dwellings. These boardwalks are large and strong enough to support many bicycles, motorcycles, and even a car for the *oba* (king),[2] all of which are novelties in Ilaje.

Given this rapid economic development, it is understandable why Olowo has been described as the most successful community development project in Nigeria (Duckworth, 1951). This assessment was made only four years after the village was founded. By 1957 it was said to have the highest standard of living of any community in the country.[3]

---

[1]According to the general census of Nigeria the population of Olowo was 1240 in 1963. According to my own census the population was 1299 in 1970. Approximately 85 of these were non-members, consisting of about 25 outsiders employed by the village and about 60 students in the community's technical school.

[2]*Oba* is the Yoruba word for king. For an analysis of the role of the *oba* among the Yoruba, see Lloyd (1954 and 1960).

[3]This observation was made by an anonymous author in *Nigeria Magazine* (1957).

A typical Olowo house.

A typical house in surrounding villages, with thatch roof and palm-rib walls.

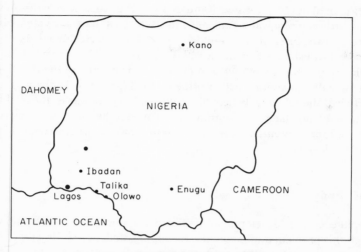

Location of Olowo and Talika in Nigeria.

In order to explain Olowo's economic success, we must consider two of its prominent features: its theocratic status and its communal social organization. As indicated, the village was founded by members of a religious sect. The Olowo people consider themselves to be Christians. They say that all their actions are conditioned by the Deity, and contend that their economic success is a direct consequence of their religious beliefs. A brief description of these beliefs, as well as an estimate of their relation to the economy, will be provided later.

The other prominent feature is the communal system. It was introduced in 1948, one year after the village was founded. From that point onward, money was not exchanged among members for goods or services. Food, clothing, and housing were provided free. In turn, members did not receive payment for working. All profits of the various industries were retained by the community leaders, to be administered as they saw fit. As will be shown later, the effects of communalism were not restricted to the economy; the organization of the family was also modified by it.

The outstanding features of Olowo are thus its rapid economic expansion, its theocratic status, and its communal social organization. Twenty years after the village was founded two radical changes occurred. First, in 1968 a small degree of private enterprise was introduced. This was antithetical to the central value system, since communalism had become the dominant feature of it. Second, in 1969 Olowo decided to extend its political influence. Many other villages in Ilaje were invited to become branches. One accepted the invitation. This political innovation was a complete reversal of the state of affairs existing prior to 1969, when the relations between Olowo and the surrounding communities were extremely hostile.

The second village that concerns us is Talika. This is a small community with a population of about 900, located 10 miles along the Atlantic coast from Olowo. Talika has little sociological significance in itself. Its importance stems from its relation to Olowo. First, it was founded in 1951 by charter members of Olowo who became disillusioned. Second, it was Talika that in 1969 accepted the invitation of Olowo to become a branch community. This in spite of the fact that there had been virtually no contact between the two villages since Talika was founded in 1951. Third, the religious beliefs of Talika are very similar to those of Olowo, but Talika does not have a communal system, nor has it industrialized. This village, therefore, is potentially useful as a control case in order to determine what made Olowo develop.

Focus of Study

The rapid economic development of Olowo has much sociological importance, but though this problem dominated my research, I shall not be directly concerned with it in the present work. Instead, the focus will be restricted to an aspect of my research that is narrower, but still of considerable significance. The focus will be upon the relationship between the structure of the economy and the family in Olowo, with comparative material drawn from Talika.

Three main problems will guide the discussion:

1. *The relationship of the communal system to the suppression of the family in Olowo.*

Communalism was introduced in 1948. This had two major consequences for the family. The first was that family ties were suppressed. Residence patterns, for example, were altered in such a way as to weaken the family. Marriage was banned for a short period, activities organized along family lines became illegitimate, and the family ceased to operate as an economic unit.

The second consequence was the emergence of family substitutes. A number of institutions and social categories began to provide functions normally associated with the family. My purpose is to demonstrate that both the suppression of the family and the emergence of family substitutes were consequences of the communal social organization, and to consider the significance of these changes for the argument that the family is universal.

2. *The relationship of the capitalist system to the legitimation of the family in Olowo.*

I have said that after about 20 years a degree of private enterprise was introduced into the village. A major consequence was that the family began to emerge as a legitimate and viable institution. Relatives started to associate with one another more openly, and the family began to operate again as an economic unit. I propose to describe the structural changes in both the economy and the family, and to show that the latter were partly a product of the former.

3. *The significance of Olowo and Talika for the body of literature concerned with the relations between economic development and family type.*

This literature contains two central propositions. One is that the nuclear family is a necessary consequence of industrialization. The other is that the extended family retards economic development.

Olowo is significant because it rejects the initial proposition. The family was suppressed for 20 years. After Olowo had rapidly expanded its economy, the extended family became stronger, and there was a sharp increase in polygyny.

Talika is significant because it rejects the second proposition. The family in Talika is of the extended family variety and unlike in Olowo has never been suppressed. As it will be argued, the nature of economic enterprise in Talika made the extended family more functional for development than the nuclear family. This is related to the greater capacity of the former to provide the labor and capital required by the economic enterprise.

The main focus, thus, is upon the relationship between changes in economic and family organization in Olowo. The relationship between the communal system and the suppression of the family will be considered in Part I. The relationship between the emergence of private enterprise and the legitimation of the family will be developed in Part II. The significance of Olowo and Talika for the two propositions concerned with the connection between family type and economic development will be focused upon in Part III. This deals most directly with the problem of Olowo's economic success, and argues that its success is partly a consequence of its family organization. No attempt will be made to present the numerous other variables, both major and minor, that contributed to Olowo's development. While this problem dominated my research, its solution is beyond the scope of the present work.

Finally, Olowo has had three *obas*. The first *oba* ruled from 1947 until his death in 1963. The second *oba* ruled from 1963 until he was overthrown during a severe illness by the present *oba* in 1966. The fact that there have been three *obas* is of great significance. For as it will be shown, most of the changes in economic and family organization coincided with periods of royal succession.

Historical Background

Olowo and Talika are located in the Okitipupa Division of Ondo Province, which in turn is in the Western State of Nigeria. This State is dominated by Yoruba-speaking people, among whom the Ilaje are included. While the Ilaje area is isolated from the Yoruba mainland, it is accessible from the sea. This may account for the fact that it came under colonial contact early. Both Britain and Germany competed for possession of it.[4]

In December 1884, the English governor and commander-in-chief of the Gold Coast arrived by ship at a seaside village within half a mile of Olowo's present

---

[4]Historical data for Ilaje are derived from a small pamphlet published in 1937 by an anonymous author. The pamphlet was probably an intelligence report prepared for the British Colonial Office.

site. A treaty of friendship was signed. A few months earlier Germany had established claim to Togo and Cameroon. In January 1885 Germany signed a treaty with the Ilaje which gave it control of the area. In June of the same year the British reacted by declaring the entire Ilaje region a protectorate. A new treaty was signed which ignored the previous German one. This was the extent of Germany's contact in Ilaje.

Ilaje-land is populated by two major ethnic groups: the Ilaje and the Ijaw. According to one myth both migrated to this area as followers of an heir to the Ile-Ife throne. Ile-Ife in Yoruba mythology is the centre of creation; all those who trace their origin to it are considered to be Yoruba. The heir is said to have lost all rights to the throne when he slept with his mother. In order to escape punishment he fled toward the safety of the swamps. At one point he ordered a large number of his subjects to settle along the river banks. These became the Ijaw. Further along he indicated where the remainder of those who had accompanied him should stay. They became the Ilaje. Over the passage of time each group is said to have assumed distinct customs and dialect. It is stressed that the account is mythological. While no satisfactory historical study has been done on this part of Nigeria, only the Ilaje are Yoruba-speaking. Further, they appear to have settled in the area earlier than the Ijaw.[5]

The Ilaje in turn are made up of two distinct peoples: the Ugbo and the Mahin. The banished prince described in the previous myth settled at a place that became known as Ugbo, and took the title of the Olugbo of Ugbo. Mahin, located about five miles from Ugbo, is ruled by the Amapetu. Both the Olugbo and the Amapetu trace their origins to the royal lineage at Ile-Ife, and are considered by their subjects to be sacred Yoruba *obas*. The Mahin throne in 1970 was unoccupied, as the result of a struggle for the succession. For this reason the Olugbo was then the dominant traditional leader of Ilaje.

Olowo was founded in 1947. It is not an isolated phenomenon. It has its roots in the Aladura (Praying) Churches, a prophetic movement widespread among the Yoruba.[6] The genesis of Olowo can be traced back to a series of reform movements among the Yoruba, commencing with the Aladuras.

The Aladuras emerged in the 1920s as a reform of Christian denominations that had been established by the early missionaries. These denominations were condemned for incorporating into them pagan beliefs and customs. The Aladuras, which eventually spread throughout West Africa, are made up of several autonomous sects. A major one is the Cherubim and Seraphim Church, founded in 1925, which penetrated into Ilaje-land about 1928. There it quickly became the domi-

---

[5]Lloyd (1957 and 1966) has referred to another Yoruba-speaking people called the Itsekiri, who live to the East of the Ilaje in the Niger Delta, as "proto-Yoruba." This term would seem to be applicable to the Ilaje as well.

[6]Peel (1968) has recently completed a study of the Aladuras in Nigeria. For a more general treatment of the Aladuras through West Africa, see Turner (1967).

nant Christian church, overshadowing denominations such as Methodist and Anglican.

The Cherubim and Seraphim Church altered the religious structure of Ilaje. However, its influence diminished as a result of another reform that took place around 1942. A number of people began to preach against a cultural practice widespread among the Ilaje: the killing of twins.[7] While the Cherubim and Seraphim Church paid lip-service to the condemnation of twin-killing, most members apparently either condoned or took part in the practice. The church, therefore, came under attack as well.

The responsibility for killing twins was held by the *oro*, a male secret society widespread both among the Yoruba on the mainland and among the Ilaje (Bascom 1969, p. 93). The strategy of those who rebelled against twin-killing was to reveal the secrets of the *oro* to the Ilaje women. The members of the *oro* were furious. They accused the rebels of disrespect for traditional customs, and attacked them physically. At the same time the Olugbo passed two laws. The first forbade two or more of the rebels to gather together at any one time. The second forced their children to leave all primary schools in Ilaje.

As a result of this persecution, those who had tried to stop twins being killed decided to establish their own village. After several unsuccessful attempts by prophets who sought to establish their right as leaders of the movement in this manner, a young man led them to a site on the land belonging to his natal village. There a new community sprang up, which became known as Olowo.

According to informants, about 2000 people joined Olowo in 1947. But only one year later the population is said to have dwindled to half of this. There were several reasons. First, they feared that government soldiers might be sent to disperse them. Second, they were not willing to fight with their relatives—often parents and siblings—in the nearby villages. Third, they were unhappy with the major innovation introduced in 1948: the communal social organization. Fourth, a number of prophets continued to seek the leadership of the village, and were forced out of Olowo for this reason.

The founding of Talika was mainly a consequence of the third and fourth reasons. The prophet who eventually established this village tried to supplant the leader of Olowo. When he failed, those who were loyal to him and disliked the communal system followed him to Talika.

Olowo and Talika, therefore, have close historical ties. Olowo emerged from the Cherubim and Seraphim Church, which was condemned for accepting the killing of twins. Talika emerged from Olowo itself. In turn, the majority of Olowo and Talika people originate from Ilaje, not from the Yoruba mainland or other parts of Nigeria. In fact 49% and 50% respectively of Olowo men and women

---

[7] As Johnson (1966, p. 25) indicates, while twin-killing no longer is widespread on the Yoruba mainland, it used to be practiced there long ago.

come from two villages within three miles.[8] Most of the remaining population are from other Ilaje villages. As regards Talika, 43% of the men come from the natal village of their leader, which is less than half a mile from Talika.[9] The origins of the women are quite different, for only 12% originate from this village. Most of the remaining men and women are from other Ilaje villages.

Finally, 93% and 81% of the current adult male and female populace respectively joined Olowo in 1947, the year the village was founded. The Talika pattern is quite different. Only 41% and 52% of the men and women joined in 1951, the year it was founded. Unlike Olowo, Talika has continued to attract recruits right up to the present. This trend reflects a difference between the villages that will have much significance for my argument: Olowo is a much more closed community.

Economy

The early settlers in Ilaje made salt from the sea and potash from mangrove trees.[10] The salt trade was abandoned in the 1930s when European salt became available. Fishing then became the major occupation. Other jobs for men were timber-cutting and palm-wine tapping, and for women the construction of mats out of raffia. Although petty trading has increased, and goods no longer are limited to staple food products such as yams, plantain, and rice, the growth of new occupations on the mainland since World War II has no counterpart in Ilaje.

It is in this context that the accomplishments of Olowo can be appreciated. It too is dependent on fishing. When the community was founded in 1947, it employed methods identical to those used by fishermen all along the coast: the men went to the sea in dug-out canoes. In a short time, though, enough funds were accumulated to allow the purchase of outboard motors and better fishing

---

[8]As will be explained in Chapter 2, Olowo is divided into male and female sectors, which consist of 137 and 156 houses respectively. With the exception of tables 1 and 2, the figures provided in the Introduction for Olowo are derived from a general questionnaire administered to all of the male sector and 76 of 156 houses in the female sector (or 49%), consisting of 429 and 197 adult men and women respectively. The questionnaire could not be completed with the remaining houses in the women's section because of the hostility it created.

[9]Talika also is divided into male and female sectors, consisting of 40 large and 121 small houses respectively. The figures for Talika throughout this study are taken from a questionnaire administered to a systematic sample of 50% of the houses in the male sector, or 20 houses containing 175 people, and a combination of a systematic and a judgment sample of 17% of the houses in the female sector, or 20 houses containing 96 people. This weaker type of sample was taken from the female sector because it was important in Talika to gather the data on entire residential sections that are presented in Chapter 8.

The technique described in the Preface was used: after the samples were selected, and a questionnaire erected excluding attitudinal variables, a trusted informant provided the answers to the various questions as they related to each person in the sample.

[10]This description of the Ilaje economy is taken from the anonymous pamphlet published in 1937.

gear. Then in 1963 the village built the first of its seven fully-mechanized sea-going trawlers. With the exception of the third (and largest) vessel, these were built with virtually no outside help. In 1969, the village imported a large ice-machine. As a result, the trawlers are able to range farther into the sea and to remain out longer, without fear of the catch spoiling.

Fishing remains the main industry of Olowo, absorbing in 1970 37% and 56% of the labor of men and women respectively. It is supported by the village's transport business. In 1955, the community built its first large launch, and since then more than 20 have been constructed. The launches carry produce and passengers throughout the Niger Delta, to Lagos to the West, and, prior to the civil war, to Cameroon to the East. As with the trawlers, the launches were built with almost no outside aid.

While the fishing and transport industries are the major sources of income in Olowo, several other enterprises exist, including boat-building, tailoring, shoe-making, weaving, and bread-making. It is not suggested that these lack importance. The boat-building department, for example, supports both the fishing and transport industries, and the launderers and bakers provide indispensable services. However, none of these occupations is a major source of income for the village.

The main sources of livelihood for Talika men are fishing and trading. Over 43% are fishermen, which is slightly more than the proportion of Olowo men who do this work. However, the real difference in the fishing industry involves the women. In Olowo 56% of the women work in the fisheries department. In Talika only 15% do so full-time. The difference reflects the much greater catch in Olowo, made possible by their seven modern, fully-mechanized trawlers.

The second major occupation among Talika men is trading. About 28% of them travel as far as Dahomey and Togo to trade. The main occupation of women is not connected with the fishing industry at all. It is the making of mats out of raffia. About half of the women do this work, including the great majority of young girls. Whereas every member of Olowo is employed in an enterprise that belongs to the community, 40% of Talika men work outside the village at least part-time. This reflects both the lesser economic activity in Talika and the lesser degree to which the village is a closed social system.

Finally, perhaps the most revealing index of the different levels of economic growth in Olowo and Talika concerns their physical structures. In Olowo there are 566 buildings, of which 294 are houses and 214 are kitchens; the latter are small buildings where the women smoke fish and prepare meals. All the houses and kitchens have tin roofs. Although not much smaller in terms of population size, Talika has only 196 buildings, of which 161 are houses and 30 are kitchens. Eighty-five of the houses and all of the kitchens have thatch roofs. Only five other buildings exist in Talika, in contrast to 58 others in Olowo; almost all of those in Olowo are part of the industrial complex: factories, sheds, and administration buildings.

Religion

Our concern is with the relationship between the economic and kinship struc-tures of Olowo and Talika, not with Olowo's economic success, nor the influence of variables such as religious beliefs on its development. Nevertheless, given the historical links of Olowo and Talika to the Aladuras, and the claims to theocratic status in both villages, a summary of the research findings concerned with the influence of religion on Olowo's economic growth,[11] and on other features, such as family organization, is warranted.

One of the problems I tried to solve during fieldwork was whether the religious beliefs of Olowo performed in a manner comparable to Weber's Protestant ethic thesis (1930). The testing procedure adopted was two-fold. The first was to examine the religious beliefs in Olowo for evidence of moral directives that might have led to economic development. This could not be done simply by measuring their beliefs against those of Calvinism. For it could not be assumed that only Calvinist beliefs could encourage development.

In a minor project the beliefs of Olowo were compared to the Calvinist ethic. The logic was as follows: given the low degree of similarity, it was doubtful that the Olowo religious beliefs contributed to development. For reasons already stated, the results of this project lack significance. The second procedure was to compare religion in Olowo to its counterpart in Talika. The logic was as follows: given a high degree of similarity, it was even less probable that religion caused Olowo's development. This is because Talika too should have industrialized, if religion had been the major cause.

The evidence initially gathered in Olowo suggested a strong connection be-tween religious beliefs and economic growth. Members of Olowo argued that faith and work are synonymous. For example, if one has work to do, there is no need to attend church services, for the act of work is an act of worship. As research progressed, however, this ideal conflicted with my observation of actual behavior in the community. As a result I concluded that there was little connection between religion and development in Olowo, in the sense of the desire for develop-ment and hard work generated by religious beliefs. Less important, it was found that there was no correspondence between their beliefs and elements of the Calvinist ethic such as predestination, individualism, and the idea of labor as a calling.

What I did find is that religion made a minor and indirect contribution to Olowo's development. First, it was a major source of social control. As the present *oba* once remarked, if his people always behaved well there would be no necessity to hold church services. Without a limit on disorder, it is unlikely that the village would have developed. Second, religious beliefs were used to provide

---

[11]This problem is dealt with in Chapters 2 and 3 of my Ph.D. thesis (Barrett 1971).

legitimacy for hard work and economic development. This was an important contribution, but not comparable to that of an independent variable.

The evidence from Talika provided further support for the conclusion that religion in Olowo was not a major cause of its economic success. Both Olowo and Talika consider themselves to be Christians, and both emerged from the Aladuras. The members from each village insist that their religious beliefs have remained the same, in spite of a separation of almost 20 years. As far as I could determine, this is correct. Both villages place special emphasis upon visions, and upon the healing power of prayers. Speaking in tongues—called angel language by some members—is also prevalent. All can be traced back to the Aladuras.

While the religious beliefs of the two villages are similar, there are two differences. The first concerns dogma. In Talika no connection is made between faith and work, even at the ideal level. The second is a difference of balance, or of degree. In Olowo religion impinges only minimally upon daily affairs; for example, services are held only once a week. In Talika, in contrast, religious beliefs dominate the affairs of the village, and services are held twice daily.

Moreover, aspects of religion that are found in both villages, such as visions, are taken much more seriously in Talika. For example, a few years ago the leader of Talika had a vision that witches were disguising themselves as pigs, and in this way escaping detection. Consequently all pigs in the village were killed. The implication of these remarks is clear: given the greater impact of the same beliefs in Talika, it is this village rather than Olowo that should have developed, if religion had been the major cause.

In sum, religious beliefs in Olowo did not *generate* the desire to industrialize, although they made development more feasible by contributing to social control and by legitimizing hard work. Further, the beliefs of Olowo and Talika are almost identical. This combined evidence strongly suggests that religion was not responsible for Olowo's economic success.

Finally, as far as I could judge, religion had almost no influence on the major changes in the Olowo family structure, nor on the family in Talika, which has been much more stable. The only exception that I am aware of occurred when the second *oba* came to the throne in 1963. He introduced a new religious goal: immortality. His argument was that this goal could only be realized if they lived an entirely communal life. For this reason he banned all marriage ties.

Power and Authority

In contrast to religion, the formal power structure of Olowo is of utmost importance in understanding the innovations in economic and family organization. Power and authority are highly centralized in the community. The vast majority of community members do not participate in decision-making. Instead, the elite imposes its will upon the populace, and failure to respond is severely punished.

The elite consists of the following 10 roles: the *oba,* the four pillars, the deputy *oba,* the bishop, the general manager of industry, the Lagos business representative, and the assistant Lagos business representative. The relative power of the ten roles correspond to the order in which they have been presented. All the roles are occupied by men. This is not accidental, for sex is a major determinant of power in the village.

The traditional Yoruba political structure also is highly centralized, consisting of about 50 kingdoms. Each kingdom has its own *oba,* who is considered to be a sacred leader. In traditional society the power of the *oba* is limited by institutional bodies such as the town chiefs and the *omole,* an informal political organization. It is of interest that Lloyd has shown that the *obas* actually increased their power during the indirect rule of the colonial period, for they were able to ignore the traditional institutional checks on their power.[12]

The *oba* is the only leadership role in Olowo that is common to the Yoruba in general. The four pillars are said to be sub-kings. They constitute as a group the most powerful members of the village with the exception of the *oba.* The *oba*'s successor is supposed to be selected from the four pillars. This procedure was followed when the first *oba* died. However, the second *oba* was overthrown by an ambitious and brilliant young man who was not among the four pillars.

The role of the deputy *oba* emerged only in 1966. It was created then by the present *oba* in order to reward a member who was instrumental in bringing him to power. This member is a relative of the *oba.* The implication is that kinship ties may be an important determinant of stratification. The results of a project undertaken to test this hypothesis will be presented later.

The bishop's power is not related to the religious realm. Indeed, he has less religious authority than the *oba* and the four pillars. Evidence for this, and for all the generalizations made about the relative power of the members of the elite, is derived from two sources. The first is a systematic examination of power in which the card-sorting technique was employed. Respondents consistently placed the bishop low in religious power. The second source is personal observation. From observation I learned that the bishop was obviously very important; for example, both young and old men would genuflect before him in the morning. But from observation I also learned that he played no major role in religion. He never delivered sermons during church services. Instead, the *oba* or the four pillars were responsible. Moreover, whenever the *oba* was absent from the village, no church service was held.

The bishop does not therefore derive his power from religion. Indeed, informants state that "bishop" is not a role, but the personal name of this man before Olowo was founded. His real power resides in his economic activity. For many years he and one of the four pillars were in charge of the community's treasury.

---

[12]Lloyd describes this in "Kings in Crisis", unpublished paper, School of Social Studies, University of Sussex.

It is relevant to add that the bishop is the brother of the first *oba,* which again suggests that it is worthwhile to investigate the hypothesis that power is reinforced through kinship. Finally, the general manager of industry is a brilliant innovator, but is not a leader of men as is the present *oba;* and the two Lagos representatives direct Olowo's commercial affairs with the outside world, but do not deliberate upon the internal fate of the village.

In addition to these 10 positions of power, there are two elite organizations in the village. One is the Supreme Council of Elders. As the name implies, a person must have reached a certain age before being eligible. The average age is 52, and the youngest member of the Council is 40. The Council consists of 30 members, including the 10 men who occupy the roles previously described. The Council meets on a regular basis, but its duties are mostly administrative. Actual policy is set by the *oba* and the four pillars, and to some extent by the other five powerful figures, outside the Council's chambers. The second organization is the Faith and Work Council of Chiefs, founded by the third *oba* in 1966. Membership is a reward for diligence, obedience, and faith, but to date it has no actual duties to perform.

Seniority is an important status principle in traditional Ilaje society,[13] as reflected in the Supreme Council of Elders. However, while not many members under 30 have much power, Olowo is by no means a gerontocracy. Capable and intelligent village members between 30–40 years of age are more likely to have power than less capable but older members.

Sex is very definitely a determinant of power in Olowo, as it is in Ilaje in general. According to the ideal belief system, the most lowly man is more important than the most powerful woman. In actuality, a handful of women do wield considerable influence. Such is the power of one of them that men genuflect in her presence. She and two other women are members of the Supreme Council of Elders. Some women have also been appointed to the Faith and Work Council. But the vast majority have little power, especially when interacting with the men, who describe them as inferior creatures. Moreover, the status and power of the women has not changed despite the village's rapid economic development.

The relation between kinship and power has special significance for us. It was revealed that the deputy *oba* is a relative of the present *oba,* and the bishop is a relative of the first *oba,* thus implying that power and kinship may be correlated. Yet this is not correct. The evidence to disprove it is drawn from a small project in which samples were taken from three status categories: high, upper-middle,

---

[13]The importance of seniority is clearly reflected in Yoruba kinship terminology. As Marris (1961, pp. 14–15) states: "Within the broad classification of relatives in general, the differences most emphasized in language are those of seniority. There is, for instance, no single Yoruba word for brother or sister, nor for sibling: the elementary terms are *egbon* for an elder sibling and *aburo* for a junior. This is because status within the family group, and in society as a whole, is largely determined by seniority, and one of the most important functions of the terms of address is to express these grades of authority." See also Bascom (1942).

and low.[14] The kinship connection of those in the samples to the three *obas* was determined. As indicated in Table 1.1, the second *oba* has far more relatives than either of the other *obas* throughout the community as a whole—19 as opposed to one for the present *oba*. The proportion is virtually the same regardless of the status category. For example, only one of the 10 members of high status is related to the present *oba*, as opposed to seven who are related to the second *oba*.

TABLE 1.1. KINSHIP AND POWER: NUMBER OF PEOPLE IN THREE
STATUS CATEGORIES RELATED BY KINSHIP TO EACH OF THE
THREE *OBAS*

	1st oba	2nd oba	3rd oba
high status (10 actors)	2	7	1
upper-middle status (12 actors)	2	4	0
low status (20 actors)	2	8	0
TOTAL	6	19	1

An additional test was made: the number of kin ties between high and upper-middle status, and high and low status, was determined. As shown in Table 1.2, the proportions are almost identical: 14% and 12% respectively. The conclusion, therefore, is that no significant correlation exists between kinship and power; if it did, the second *oba* might not have been overthrown. The explanation for the lack of correlation is clear: it has to do with the manner in which the family has been suppressed. Any effort to help one's relatives is considered to be deviant. As informants stress, whenever one is in trouble, he can never ask a relative to intervene. To do so would set the odds fully against him from the outset.

---

[14]These samples were drawn entirely from the male sector. High status was defined in two ways. The first was objective. Only those members who belonged to the Supreme Council of Elders or to the Faith and Work Council of Chiefs were eligible. These consisted of 46 men. The second method was impressionistic. Only what I termed the inner circle of power among the 46 was selected. This consisted of 10 men. Since the number was small, all 10 were retained rather than a sample.

The next category was termed upper-middle in order to suggest that it was not far below the status of the first category. Upper-middle status included all those who were members of the Supreme Council of Elders and Faith and Work, but who were not included in the first category. These consisted of 36 men. A simple random sample of 12, or 33%, was selected.

Low status was defined as all those men who were not members of the Supreme Council of Elders, or Faith and Work, not leaders of their line, had one wife or less, and were over 40 years of age. It was discovered in a previous project that the leaders of the lines, a social category that will be described in Chapter 3, occupied a middle-range status. It also was found that the number of wives possessed varied not only with status, but with age as well, which made controls for it necessary too. Ninety-five people qualified for the category. A simple random sample was selected of 20 of them, or 20%.

TABLE 1.2. KINSHIP AND POWER: NUMBER OF KIN
RELATIONSHIPS BETWEEN (A) HIGH AND UPPER-MIDDLE
AND (B) HIGH AND LOW STATUS

	high status (n)	10 actors (%)
(a) upper-middle status (12 actors)	17	14[a]
(b) low status (20 actors)	23	12[b]

[a]Total possible relationships = 120 (10 × 12).
[b]Total possible relationships = 200 (10 × 20).

In Talika there is also an elite. This consists of about eight prophets (all men), and includes one person who is called *oba,* as in Olowo. Their control over the village, however, is not nearly as extensive as in Olowo. Their major duty is to provide religious inspiration and protection for the villagers, who are constantly threatened by witches.

The elite does not take much interest in the economic affairs of the villagers, who are free to work when and where they want. They also are at liberty to leave the village without the permission of the *oba,* except when calamity strikes, such as an outbreak of witchcraft. This is in sharp contrast to Olowo. There the daily activity of the people is regulated by the elite. A person's job, choice of spouse, and education are decided by those in power. Moreover, a person is severely punished for leaving the village without permission. This again suggests that Olowo is a much more closed social system. This factor, in conjunction with the more authoritarian leadership style in Olowo, is important in understanding its greater experimentation with economic and family organization.

Part One

COMMUNALISM AND THE SUPPRESSION OF THE FAMILY

---

2. The Communal System

Communalism and Community Defined

Olowo was founded in 1947. One year later an outstanding innovation was introduced—the communal social organization. Before describing the communal system, I shall indicate what it means to Olowo people. Some of the well-educated members use the term "communism" to describe their village. By this they do not imply any connection to international politics. Communism instead refers to the social organization of the village. The majority of members do not use this term. Instead they describe Olowo as a "community." "Community" in this sense does not mean a village or a town, but refers instead to both ideology and social organization.

In relation to ideology, the term "community" has the connotations of equality for all members and the subordination of the individual to the collective. While most members do enjoy a similar standard of living, there is considerable power differentiation. This differentiation is so great that "community" in reality does not mean the subordination of the individual to the collective as much as it means the subordination of the collective to the elite.

Over the years, "community" eventually became the central feature of the village value system. This is evident from the tendency of members to use "community" in a religious sense. For example, they often state that regardless of the presence of Cherubim and Seraphim or other churches in the nearby villages, the outsiders have no religion. This must follow, argue Olowo members, for these villages are not organized along communal lines.

In order to avoid confusion, I shall not use "community" as a synonym for communalism or communism. Instead I shall employ it to mean a village or town.

Communalism is also used by members of Olowo to refer to their social organization. The two structures most affected by the communal innovation are the economy and the family. These structures began to change at approximately the same time. Nevertheless, I shall argue that communalism in Olowo is primarily an economic phenomenon. Support for this argument is drawn from both attitudes and social structure, although a discussion of the latter must wait until the precise nature of economic and family change has been described.

As regards attitudes, the major goal of the village is to industrialize, not to

19

realize a specific type of family organization. Evidence of this is provided almost daily in the village. Members talk about what must be done to accelerate economic growth. Almost never do they discuss family affairs, let alone speculate about an ideal family form. The communal system is intended as a means to realize the economic goals. The suppression of the family is also addressed to these goals. It contributes indirectly to them by not hindering the communal structure of the economy.

Communalism, then, is more of an economic than a family phenomenon, and in turn contrasts with capitalism. It would be difficult to provide a thorough definition of these economic philosophies in a few sentences. However, the following brief definitions may serve to clarify the argument. The following minimal characteristics of capitalism exist in Ilaje: there is private ownership; labor is an individual affair in the sense that while operating within a structure of social relations (or an organization, such as the Ilaje Women's Fish Association) a person is oriented primarily to his own gratification rather than to that of the collectivity; and profits are retained by the individual.

The following minimal characteristics of communalism exist in Olowo: there is no private ownership; labor is a collective affair; all profits are retained by the central treasury, to be administered as the leaders see fit. What I want to show is that shortly after Olowo was founded, the components of capitalism that dominate Ilaje society were replaced by those of communalism. What I shall show in Part II is that this process was partially reversed after the third *oba* assumed office: capitalism was revived.

The Economy

According to members of Olowo, before the village was founded in 1947 they had no plan to adopt communalism. A decision to do so was made approximately a year later. As a result of the decision, all personal possessions were turned over to the community. This included watches, rings, and cash. Even clothing became communal property: wealthy members who had brought with them several garments were allowed to keep only one. The remainder was put at the disposal of the village leaders, to be distributed among those who were in need.

From this point onward no money was exchanged among members for goods or services, work became a collective affair with men and women toiling in large gangs, and all profits went to the community treasury. In turn, the community assumed responsibility for basic necessities. Members did not pay for food, clothing, or housing. In order to facilitate the distribution of goods, two buildings were set aside. One was called the community shop. It stocked flashlight batteries, soap, and other minor items. While these were provided without payment, members report that it was difficult to acquire the goods, for those who were in charge would only release them if one could present a convincing argument.

The second building contained more substantial goods, such as clothing. Periodically these were distributed to all members of the community. If one needed an item, such as a shirt, it was not necessary to wait until the general day of distribution. However, a request would only be granted if it was supported by one of the village leaders. In addition to these services, the community paid the fees for several young people who were sent to schools on the mainland, and provided the expenses for others who had a legitimate purpose to travel outside the village.

At first fishing was the only industry. Gradually several other enterprises were established. These included boatbuilding, shoe making, tailoring, and baking. As the several new industries were introduced, the organization of work was modified. Three distinct patterns emerged. The most important involved the adoption of the department as the main unit of administration. Each factory and other major industry such as fishing, carpentry, and boatbuilding became a separate department. All adult members of both sexes were assigned to a particular department. Even children of primary school age were included under this organizational unit. After school was closed at 2 P.M. each child had to report to a specific department.

The second pattern of work was carried out in large gangs. This was the dominant type at the beginning. With the emergence of the department its importance declined, but did not disappear. Communal labor continued to occur whenever there was a job to do that was either too big for a particular department, or not the direct responsibility of any department. As an example of the initial case, members often were summoned to help draw the fishing trawlers onto land for repairs. As an example of the second case, the entire community periodically gathered to cut grass and weeds that grew around the town. Such labor occurs now on an average of twice a week in the dry season.

A third pattern of work was not formally organized at all. It involved individual labor. For example, before the factories opened in the morning a person would go to the seashore to catch fish, which then were dried or smoked. What was not consumed was sold to strangers in the community market, or in nearby villages. Some members also kept chickens and ducks or attempted to grow oranges and bananas. This was the only type of work in Olowo that was not a collective enterprise.

In spite of the changes in organization of work, there was no modification of the system of rewards. In the case of the departments all profits were regularly turned over to the community. This occurred at the end of each month, when a bell was rung. Then a representative of each department took the money to the treasury of the village. Also, those members who had earned a pound or two from individual effort, such as fishing at the seashore, gave their earnings to the treasury. Since communal labor never resulted in any profit, it posed no problem when the new patterns of work emerged.

The Family

At approximately the same time that the structure of the economy was modified along communal lines, the suppression of the family began. Before describing how this was done, two tasks must be undertaken. The first is to define the main kinship units referred to in this study: the nuclear, polygamous, and extended families.

The nuclear family "consists typically of a married man and woman with their offspring . . ." (Murdock, 1966, p. 1). This type is supposedly dominant in Western society.[1] A polygamous family "consists of two or more nuclear families affiliated by plural marriages" (Murdock, 1966, p. 2), i.e., in the Ilaje case by having the husband in common. An extended family "consists of two or more nuclear families affiliated through an extension of the parent-child relationship rather than of the husband-wife relationship, i.e., by joining the nuclear family of a married adult to that of his parents." (Murdock, 1966, p.2) The Ilaje family is both polygamous and extended. When it is said that the Olowo family has changed, it is this baseline that is being used.

The second task is to make explicit three assumptions concerning the Olowo family. The initial one is made by both members of Olowo and their immediate neighbours, and the other two are of a sociological nature.

Assumption 1: *The family in Olowo does not exist, and hence is not relevant for social behavior.*

While I agree that social activities were not organized according to family ties, I shall argue strongly against the claim that the family does not exist. As will be shown, since Olowo was founded a certain percentage of close relatives have lived together, and for most of the reign of the first *oba* a formal marital bond existed.

Assumption 2: *During the reigns of the first and second obas the family was even LESS important than suggested by its structural properties, and during the reign of the third oba is even MORE important than these suggest.*

The relevant structural properties are the number of relatives living together, and the presence or absence of a formal marital bond. As will be shown in Part II, the family has become structurally stronger since 1966, when the third *oba* assumed office. However, the change in structure is not an accurate index of the degree to which the family has become a major principle of social organization.

The purpose of the third assumption is to capture the significance of the family in Olowo at present.

Assumption 3: *Since 1966 there has been a shift from kinship identification to kinship consciousness.*

Kinship identification has always been present in Olowo. That is, while activi-

---

[1]This note of doubt is intentional. As will be shown in Chapter 8, recent research suggests that the nuclear family is not as typical of Western society as formerly assumed.

ties were not organized according to family membership, people were aware of the identity of their relatives. Since 1966 there has been a shift from kinship identity to kinship consciousness. That is, in spite of the fact that a large proportion of relatives continue to live apart, members have begun to organize their social and economic activities according to their family membership, and to shift their allegiance from the community to the family. Because data on family organization since the reign of the third *oba* are not given until Part II, it will not be possible to develop the latter half of the second and third assumptions until that time.

Marriage

It has been explained that wealthy members with several garments had to turn all except one over to the community when communalism was introduced in 1948. At the same time wealthy men with two or more wives were asked to keep the one of their choice and turn the others over to the community. These were then distributed among men who had no wife. This arrangement only lasted a couple of years. According to nonmembers it was discarded because of the taunts from surrounding villagers. They state that most of the old men kept their young wives, relinquishing their more mature ones for the single men. These young men were then teased for sleeping with their mothers.

A more plausible explanation concerns the attempt to establish communalism. The distribution of wives gave way to a system of common marriage. More precisely, there was no marriage at all. Adults were allowed to have sexual access to anyone of the opposite sex. The communal love system did not endure. I am not certain why this was so. Nor can I say with confidence exactly what followed. Informants agreed that it was replaced by a system of formal marriage within a year or so. Some stated that the formal relation persisted until the second *oba* came to the throne in 1963. Others argued that it collapsed again after about a year, was briefly replaced by a communal love system once more, and then resumed until the first *oba* died.

Part of the confusion is connected with the initial distribution of women among single men. Some informants interpreted this as a communal marriage system, although it was quite different from the arrangement in which all marital ties were forbidden. It is my impression that at the beginning marriage was banned only on one occasion. Those who stated that it was banned twice confused the initial system of distribution with the communal love system.

Considerable change thus took place in marital arrangements shortly after Olowo was founded. But a fairly stable system gradually emerged, and husband and wife were recognized as forming a permanent bond. The choice of partner did not belong to the individual. The *oba* reserved the right to donate wives to men who were eligible. Further, there was no ceremony, no ritual. The *oba* simply announced that a man and woman were married. It has been suggested by members that men had minimal choice in their partners, but women none. Some cases have been uncovered, however, in which men left the community because of unhappiness with the spouse who was forced upon them.

It is important to stress that after the formal marital bond was established the majority of men took only one wife. (see Table 6.2). This was not because of a policy of monogamy. It was due partly to the ideal of equality, but more to a shortage of women. Indeed, many men eligible for marriage did not have wives. Women were scarce for a number of reasons. One was that apparently less women than men had joined Olowo at the beginning. Second, numerous women escaped from the community. Men left as well, but according to both member and nonmember informants many of the men but few of the women returned. Third, there was a policy of nonrecruitment of outsiders, although that policy has been modified since the present *oba* assumed control: outside women are now welcomed—but not men. Finally an exception to the forced monogamy concerns the *obas*. The first *oba* had more than 30 wives; the second *oba* had two wives; the third *oba* had 14 wives.

The first *oba* died in 1963. His successor was a man who had sought the leadership of the movement prior to the founding of Olowo, but who had lost out to the first *oba*. It is clear that an uneasy peace had existed between them over the years. As evidence, the second *oba* ordered all pictures of his predecessor to be destroyed. He also reversed many of the policies of the first *oba,* or revived ones that long ago had disappeared.

An example of the latter concerns marriage. The second *oba* banned marriage ties as had been done around 1950. Supposedly he did this in order to help realize a religious goal that he made popular: immortality. His argument was that this goal could be attained only by increasing the range of communalism. Once more we see that communalism has a religious connotation in Olowo. It is significant that not one informant referred positively to the dissolution of marriage. They said that it resulted in chaos. This was primarily manifested in the relations between men and women, who fought for each other's favours. It also concerned the economy. People apparently did not report to their departments in the morning. One informant explained that this was because they were exhausted by sexual activity. It may actually have been a result of the general disorder in the village.

Somewhat irrelevantly, this same informant said that the women were much more active than the men in seeking a number of sexual partners. While I did not verify his statement from the accounts of other informants, it is compatible with a dominant attitude of Olowo men toward their women: they consider them immoral. Finally, venereal disease is reported to have been widespread during this period. Once again I have no way of verifying this information.

To conclude, the reign of the second *oba* was one of disorder. A great many people are said to have left the village at this time. Some members claimed that when the third *oba* came to the throne in 1966 the village was on the verge of disintegration. Deciding that one of the major sources of strain was the absence of marriage, he reintroduced a formal marital bond. It will be described in Chapter 5.

Child-Rearing

The system of child-rearing in Olowo differs in two main ways from that in Ilaje in general. First, a kindergarten was established in 1954. All children three through five years old are kept there during the day, allowing their parents to work unhindered. It also contributes to the communal ideology: children are placed in a collective situation at an early age.

The second difference is again related to the communal system. It is the policy of the village that children should not be raised by their own parents. At the age of five or six all children are supposed to move to the house of another adult, who becomes their master. According to members there is a sound reason for the policy. They argue that it is much easier to punish another's child rather than one's own. Thus their system is conducive to the objective training of children. The policy also contributes to the communal ideology, for the children belong to the community, not to their own parents.

How was it decided where a child of either sex should live after the age of five or six? This was not a problem. Adults simply went to the kindergarten and claimed a child. The two men in charge of the kindergarten had the authority to donate a child to an adult who made a request. Often there was no reason for selecting a particular child. As some informants stressed, this was irrelevant inasmuch as a child was wanted in order to perform as a servant. It would seem that their observation is too harsh. Other members stated that a child and an adult may have grown fond of each other through association, and this would explain the adult's choice. Or two people may have been good friends. As a token of their friendship they requested each other's children from the men in charge of the kindergarten.

Residence Patterns

One feature of residence in Olowo stands out: the entire village is split into male and female sectors, separated by a central boardwalk. Husband and wife do not live together. Instead, three or four men will live in one house in the male sector, and their mates will live with three or four women in houses in the female sector. This arrangement is highly atypical of Ilaje. It is customary for a wealthy man to live separately from his wives, each of whom may have a small house of her own. But a husband and his wives constitute a compound. They do not live in different sectors of the village.

The division of Olowo into male and female sectors affects child-rearing practices as well as the marital bond. Children of both sexes remain with their own mother until the age of five or six. At that age all children supposedly move to the house of another adult, who becomes the child's master. Thus girls move to another house in the female sector, while boys move across to the male sector, but not to their father's house. While I lack precise figures for the period prior to the reign of the present *oba,* it appears that a few boys moved into their father's house in the male sector, while even more girls did not leave their mother's house at all. The policy, therefore, was not enforced absolutely (see Tables 6.4 and 6.5).

The apparently obvious explanation of this division is that by dividing the village in this manner, the family was weakened, and thus interfered less with the communal system. But the members of Olowo insist that the reasons are more environmental than social, and concern the basic livelihood of the community: the fishing industry.

It is the men's job to catch the fish, and the women's job to process them. Because of the absence of refrigeration, the catch must be smoked or dried. At the beginning this was done inside the dwellings themselves, as is normal in Ilaje. This was unsatisfactory, for the houses were constantly filled with smoke and with the odor of fish. Moreover, houses at times caught on fire. For these reasons the community decided to move all the women to the interior side of the town, which was downwind. Men who had been living at that side of the town crossed over to what became the male side. Later the women complained that they did not like the smoke, the smell, or the threat of fire. As a result, special huts or kitchens were built, where the fish could be processed. In 1969 there were 214 of these kitchens.

When Olowo was first founded, male and female lived together. It was not until 1953 that a separate section was created for each sex. Given the time lag between this innovation and the introduction of communalism in 1948, the people's own explanation of the division must be taken seriously. Nevertheless, it is reasonable to argue that if the division was not entirely stimulated by social factors, the latter were at least partly responsible, for the division is a variation on the communal theme.

Quite apart from the causes of the division, the consequences for the family were significant. Not only was the affinal link dislocated, but also the relationship between parents and children, between children of the opposite sex after they reached the age of five or six, and often between children of the same sex, since they were distributed among different houses.

In concluding, let us consider the three assumptions made earlier in the chapter. The first is that in Olowo the family does not exist, and thus is not relevant to social behavior. Both members of Olowo and their neighbors argue in this vein. We have seen that major structural changes have occurred to reduce the importance of the family. This result also was achieved by other means. For example, members were given new names. This has prompted ridicule from the surrounding villagers. They claim that the community attempts to disguise the identity of those who join, and that as a result nobody in Olowo knows to whom he is related.

As regards their initial claim, the present *oba* himself recently has mocked the practice of renaming members. During a church service in 1970 he suggested that such practices are out-dated in the community. With respect to the second claim, the outsiders are in error. Although no formal activity is organized along kinship lines, members do know the identity of their relatives. This first was impressed

Main boardwalk in Olowo, separating the male and female sectors.

A nearby village, without the advantage of boardwalks.

upon me when observing cases of conflict. As I learned, it is the responsibility of the kin group to punish those who misbehave. Thus, whenever anybody makes a "mistake," such as adultery or theft, the kin group emerges as a visible entity. The connection of the family to conflict also became clear when I began to work with an informant on kinship. At one point I expressed surprise at his detailed knowledge of the family connections among members. His response was that one is always reminded of these relations when a deviant is being punished.

A further factor that contradicts the assumption that the family does not exist is that there was no systematic attempt to eradicate the family completely. For most of the initial 20 years a formal marital bond existed, and a certain proportion of members of the same sex lived in a house with at least one other relative. Thus, although largely invisible in terms of social action conditional by it, and structurally fragmented, the family was not destroyed.

It is not only outsiders who claim the family is nonexistent in Olowo. Members of the village themselves often boast that their community spirit is so strong that family ties are meaningless. They support this claim by referring to the many battles in the beginning with relatives in nearby villages who did not join the community. Even in 1970 there was evidence of dissociation from relatives outside the village. For example, a young woman was granted permission to visit her father in a nearby village for the first time since Olowo was founded. She declined. Her reason was that since her father had shown no interest in her over the years, she should show no interest in him.

However, contrary evidence did emerge during the course of fieldwork. This concerns the members who "escape" from Olowo. As indicated, many of these rejoin the community, and the reason given by most of them is that their parents, or spouse and children, are still in Olowo. The implication is that Olowo people are correct in claiming that family ties with nonmembers are unimportant. But they are wrong to claim that they have been able to eradicate family ties completely. For within the village members are aware of the identity of their relatives, and escapees even return to the community in order to be with their families.

This evidence also supports the initial part of the second assumption: that the importance of the family was even less at the beginning than suggested by its structural properties. For while a certain proportion of relatives of the same sex lived together, and a formal marital bond existed most of the time, the family was not a legitimate unit of social organization. Evidence for the latter part of this assumption and for the third assumption must wait until Part II, where it will be shown that kinship consciousness now is endemic in the village.

3. Family Substitutes

The pattern of economic and family change during the early years in Olowo consists of a causal chain with three links. The first is the introduction of communalism and the second is the suppression of the family, which were discussed in the previous chapter. The third is the emergence of family substitutes; that is, structures that act as functional alternatives to the family. The existence of these substitutes has negative significance for Murdock (1966), who argues that the family is universal. But it has positive significance for Spiro (1963), who describes similar substitutes in the kibbutz, and challenges Murdock's thesis. The implications of the Olowo case for the work of both authors will be considered in the next chapter. My purpose now is to describe several structures that appear to serve family functions.

Two criticisms come immediately to mind. The preceding comments assume that the functions normally provided by the family can be identified. What, in fact, are these, and which of them were provided outside the family in Olowo? Murdock contends not only that the family is universal, but that it always has four functions: sexual, reproductive, economic, and educational (Murdock, 1966, p. 3). By educational he means child-rearing and socialization. In the next chapter it will be shown that at varying times and in varying degrees all four functions have been performed outside the family. However, my concern here is with the educational function. I shall try to show that in Olowo the primary provision for this function has fallen to extra-family structures.

One factor must be stressed. It is not argued that the family makes no contribution to child-rearing and socialization. As indicated in the previous chapter, children live with their own mothers until the age of five or six. Even after this age, some children remain with their own mothers or fathers. What I do argue is that the child-rearing and socialization function is *predominantly* served outside the family. This is especially the case as the child grows older.

The second criticism is that to look outside the family for the provision of functions normally provided by the family is to assume that the function is indispensible. I obviously do make this assumption. This in itself is without fault, for as Spiro has remarked (1954, p. 839), the four functions that Murdock associates with the family are prerequisites for the maintenance of any society.

This does not mean I also assume *structural* indispensibility. As it has been stressed by Durkheim long ago (1938), and by Radcliffe-Brown (1961) and Levy

(1952) more recently, the same structures in different societies can perform different functions, and different structures in different societies can perform the same functions. My argument, indeed, supports their position: in Olowo functions often associated with the family are provided by other structures. These include the kindergarten, the landlord, the line,[1] the department, and the community as an entity.

The Kindergarten

Beginning our discussion with the kindergarten will place the argument in proper perspective, because the kindergarten has not replaced the family in child-rearing and socialization, but rather has assumed part of the responsibility for this function.

The kindergarten was founded in 1953. All children between the ages of two to five attend. They spend the entire day at the kindergarten, returning to their own dwellings in the evening. No comparable institution exists in Ilaje. Children in the surrounding villages are cared for by their mothers or by other female adults such as the mothers' co-wives. Older children are looked after by older brothers and sisters.

The kindergarten is under the direction of two men, who are aided by several women. From my observation, little effort is made to teach the children skills or academic material. Even the games that are played do not seem to have a didactic element. This may simply be a result of the fact that the two men in charge are elderly and uneducated. They could have been replaced, however, by well-educated young women or men. It is relevant to add that the Olowo kindergarten is very different from the kibbutz nursery, where the emphasis is upon task-orientation and performance (Talmon, 1965).

While very few skills are taught to the children, those in charge appear to have two goals in mind. One is to keep the children quiet. This is done by lightly flogging them with small gads. Flogging is widespread at the adult level, and thus the children are being prepared for the future. A second goal is the suppression of individual expression. The children are encouraged to play, eat, and sleep together. Even at activities outside the kindergarten, such as church services, the children were grouped together and watched over by those in charge of the kindergarten. With the exception of the present *oba*'s own son, rarely did I observe a child being singled out and asked to perform. On the contrary, the entire kindergarten will occasionally march around the village, stopping at the residence of an important member to sing his or her praises.

Since I am not a psychologist, I hesitate to generalize about the mental health

---

[1]Both "line" and "bridge" are used as synonyms for "street" in the village. For clarity, I shall only use "line."

of the children. My impression was that as reported for other communal settlements such as the kibbutz (Irvine, 1952), the collective upbringing of the children in Olowo has not done them any harm. I am even more reluctant to employ concepts such as *n* Achievement and *n* Affiliation to describe the personality of these children. Even if able to do so, I would not want to make further assumptions about the linkage to economic development, as McClelland (1967) and LeVine (1966) do. My own suspicion is that quite contrary to what these authors assume, the stress on obedience and collectivism will not result in a personality type that will limit the future development of the village. As Bennett has remarked in his work with the Hutterites (1967), achievement and collectivity orientation are not necessarily contradictory.

Olowo members explain that the kindergarten was founded in order that women could work unimpeded by their children. This is probably correct. But the kindergarten has assumed part of the responsibility of socializing the children. This is obvious by virtue of the fact that the children spend all day away from their parents. But the contribution of the kindergarten also is a result of the peculiar values that dominate it. The emphasis upon obedience and the suppression of individualism condition the youth into acceptance of the communal system.

Landlords and Landladies

A second category that has semi-family functions is that of the landlord and landlady. While houses are not owned by individuals in Olowo, the *oba* appoints one person to be in charge of each dwelling. This usually is an older member (the average age of the landlords and landladies respectively is 52 and 51). While the position of landlord is not one of high status, a younger man who is very important will occasionally be appointed over older men of lower status.

As it will be shown in Part II, residence is quite stable among adults. One moves to another house mainly for two reasons: the house is over-crowded, or a person makes a "mistake," as deviance is called in the community. Movement for the second reason is confined primarily to young people, whose mistake most often concerns adultery. However, it sometimes occurs among older people. For example, during my period of fieldwork a middle-aged man who was accused of witchcraft was moved to another house where his behavior could be observed by the landlord.

Because of the minimal residence changes, landlords become identified with a particular house, and for all intents and purposes can be considered to own it. This makes the role of the landlord very important as regards the socialization function. As it has been shown, children are distributed among nonrelatives in the village, and the landlord is responsible for training the children who live in his house. The latter are responsible for washing clothes, carrying water, etc., and address the landlord as "master" or "father." The landlord is said to be better equipped to train a child than the parents because he will not hesitate to apply physical punishment when necessary.

The importance of the landlord and the landlady with respect to socialization is reflected in the case of newcomers. When one joins Olowo, one is at once assigned to a landlord or landlady, who is addressed as "my father" or "my mother." The landlord or landlady then assumes responsibility for teaching the newcomer how to behave in the village.

Finally, my impression is that the relationship between landlord (or landlady) and child is not often one of intimacy. Indeed, some cases were observed in which the prevailing attitude was hostility. For example, one young man continually made trouble for his landlord, who was considered to be a gentle man, and not deserving such treatment. But such cases are extreme. I think that the relationship between landlord and child is essentially one of impersonality, of a lack of emotion—either hostile or friendly. The implication is that while the landlord and landlady contribute to the socialization of the child, and provide the latter with a long-range identity to a specific household, they do not provide intimacy. This was implied in the earlier observation that the landlord and landlady are better equipped to train the child than the latter's parents. They are better equipped in the sense that they do not have an emotional attachment to the child.

The Line and Line Leader

The third social category that seems to provide semifamily functions is the line and the line leader. It has been explained that a few years after Olowo was founded the entire village was split into male and female sectors, separated by a central boardwalk. When this occurred, the basic physical structure of the village that existed in 1970 was established. The two sectors in turn contain 20 smaller boardwalks at right angles to the central walk. On either side of the walks, all of which sit on stilts, there are eight to 10 houses. Each of these walks is called a line.

It is not likely that the line had any significance at the beginning other than as a residential unit. However, as time went by each line developed its own social identity, and a great number of activities, such as communal work, began to be organized according to lines. For example, the village recently undertook an ambitious project to build roads by piling mud together, rather than by constructing boardwalks. These roads quickly overgrow with grass. Each line in the village has been assigned a section of the road, with the responsibility of keeping the grass cut.

It is not only in cases of work that the line acts as a collectivity. Social events often are arranged according to lines. For example, during 1970 a grand celebration took place in the palace courtyard in order to honor the *oba*'s most recent marriage. At this celebration all those living in the same line sat together. Moreover, chairs, tables, food, and beverages were provided by the line residents themselves.

Lines sometimes hold parties. Residents of other lines are not excluded, but must be invited. While parties are more frequent on the male than on the female side, women usually join their husbands during these occasions. This is compatible with the normal interaction between men and women in Olowo. When they interact it is almost always on the male side. The women cross over to the male sector to bring food, to visit, for parties, and for sex.

The line, thus, has emerged as a cohesive social unit. This was a gradual process, and probably was a result of the sheer physical nature of the line: the proximity of members to each other in a clearly defined territory. But it was also due to deliberate community policy. The line had great potential as a unit of administration. This was recognized by the first *oba,* for in 1957 he appointed a leader to each line. While this role was not formally established until 1957, informants state that informal leaders had emerged before then. Thus the action of the *oba* was basically to provide legitimacy to leadership.

The most important function of the leader of the line concerns social control. In terms of power and status, the line leader occupies only a middle-range position. But because of his strategic location in the community, he quickly learns about most cases of trouble and conflict. He must decide whether to solve the problem himself, or to send it further up the authority structure to the deputy *oba,* the four pillars, or the *oba.* Unless the problem is severe—such as an attempt by a member to "escape" from the village—the leader will try to solve it himself.

Each line in the female sector also has a leader, whose duties are supposedly identical to her male counterpart. It is correct that she organizes the residents in the line for communal work, and is responsible for their behavior. However, the female line leaders are subordinate to the male leaders. Indeed, when a problem arises that cannot be solved by the female leader, she does not go to a member of the elite. Instead, she goes to the male leader in the line opposite her own. He in turn decides what must be done. This pattern reinforces the earlier assumption that women are considered inferior to men in Olowo.

In concluding, I want to make clear the relation between the line and the family. Which of these has the greater influence over the individual? The answer to this question is not straightforward, because it depends upon the circumstances confronting the individual. Suppose, for example, that a young man has committed adultery. If members of his family discover his "mistake," they will not usually inform someone in authority such as the line leader. But if the leader of the line learns about the "mistake" and decides to punish the deviant, the latter's family do not try to protect him. Indeed, the members of his family will flog him more severely than will anybody else. For this reason it is necessary for the line leaders to caution them to be moderate. Because of this excess punishment, the present *oba* has said that the part played by the kin group in punishing offenders must be reduced.

The relative influence of the line and the family, then, depends upon the circumstances. If the "mistake" is known only among a person's family, the latter may condone it, or even cooperate. Some cases of this were uncovered during fieldwork. But when the deviance becomes manifest all relatives must take part in the public ritual of punishment. Their overreaction would seem to be an attempt to show that kin ties are unimportant. But in effect it is proof that they are, for their actions are prompted by the reflected shame that they feel as a result of their relative's behavior.

The line and the line leader, therefore, have outstanding significance for my thesis. The line is a major instrument of social control and a source of solidarity for the individual. Indeed, the entire line can be said to function as a large extended family. The tendency for a person's family unit to take priority over the line under certain circumstances also is significant. It stresses once again that structures such as the line do not replace the family. Instead they assume part of its functions.

The Department

A fourth structure that may act as a family substitute is the department. It constitutes the major mechanism for organizing work in the village. Every adult member belongs to a specific department. As stated before, even primary school students are assigned to a department, where they are expected to report after school finishes at 2 P.M. While the actual contribution of the children is minor, their presence is required for two reasons. One is to run messages for the regular workers. The other is to condition them to the values of hard work in a collective atmosphere. As the manager of the tailoring department once remarked, it is important to expose them to these values while they are young.

A department is more than an impersonal place of work. As in the case of the line, it is a major focus of identity for the individual. One of the first facts a member of Olowo will reveal about himself is the department to which he belongs.

Just as the leader of the line contributed to line solidarity, the manager of the department operates in a similar manner. The relation between manager and worker is diffuse. The latter expects guidance from his manager about a wide range of matters, such as marriage and illness. The importance of the manager in realms beyond work was impressed upon me when investigating residence patterns. A case arose that baffled explanation. I almost concluded that residence was random, or at least not related to factors that I could detect. But an informant then told me that the member in question was living with his manager. This, of course, is only one case. Yet the readiness of the informant to accept the connection of worker to manager as a reasonable explanation is significant.

It would be an exaggeration to describe the manager as a father surrogate. But at the same time there is a tendency for the manager to approximate this role. This tendency is not a result of particular personalities. It is a normative pattern built into the role of the manager itself.

While the department, then, is less important than the line with respect to family functions, it remains significant. This is because the village employs it intentionally to socialize children to the values of hard work and cooperation. Further, it is a focus of identification for members. Finally, it is characterized by expressive behavior that far exceeds the specific requirements for task performance.

A last potential alternative to the family is the community as an entity. When asked what family they belong to, members of Olowo sometimes respond that the community is their family. In a sense this is not an exaggeration. The identification of the individual with the community is again comparable to the relation of an Ilaje resident to his extended family. Contributing to the primacy of the community as a focus of identification is the tendency of members to use "community" in a religious sense. This reflects the degree to which it occupies a central position in the ideology of the village. Identification with the community is especially strong during periods of conflict with the surrounding villages. In a psychological sense, then, the community can be said to function like a large extended family. As shown in the next chapter, Spiro makes the same claim for the kibbutz.

Conclusion

The early physical care and later socialization of the child is a functional requisite of any society. Unless Olowo is to depend solely upon the recruitment of outsiders (which it does not), it is also a requisite of the village. Because the family has been suppressed, this function must be provided by some other structure or combination of structures. This accounts for the emergence of family substitutes in Olowo.

In conclusion, two other interpretations of the tendency of these structures to act as substitutes to the family will be considered. First, my argument has been that this is a result of the suppression of the family. Inasmuch as the latter is a consequence of the communal system, the substitutes are indirect consequences as well. The tendency for these structures to assume a socializing function may also be *directly* related to the communal system: they are employed to reinforce the ideology of communalism. This function has nothing to do with universal family requisites. It is related instead to the peculiar nature of the village itself. If this is the case, the emergence of family substitutes is generated from two sources: the suppression of the family, and the communal system. But both are ultimately connected with communalism: the first indirectly, the second directly.

The other interpretation concerns a basic psychological condition. Can the emergence of family substitutes be interpreted as a need for solidarity? By solidarity I mean identity and intimacy. These represent two points on a continuum. With the exception of the community as an entity, the family substitutes broke down the primary interaction within the village into smaller units. In this way they provided members with a series of identities. In a criss-crossing fashion, these would tend to cement the members into an overall state of solidarity.

Very little evidence, however, was found of intimacy in connection with the family substitutes. As was shown, the relation between the landlord and child is one of impersonality. The only structure that did seem to foster intimacy was the kindergarten. There a child could play with his peers.

Talmon (1965, p. 278) states that the suppression of the family in the kibbutz has not disrupted family solidarity. On the contrary, emotional ties between parents and children have been strengthened, partly because parents do not have the responsibility of disciplining their children. While this is a highly subjective judgment, I do not think that the suppression of the family has had a comparable effect in Olowo. Instead it has placed people in that grey area between community and family identification, which results in a diffusion of intimacy. There are, however, signs that this has begun to change. Yet the growing intimacy among close relatives described in Part II has not coincided with family suppression, but is a direct consequence of the relaxation of pressures against family interaction.

At this juncture it is relevant to reveal the existence of numerous face-to-face groups within Olowo. These include several musical groups, a Boy Scout organization, a Red Cross society, and women's organizations. These groups differ from the family substitutes inasmuch as they do not impinge upon every member of the village, but in each case are restricted to a handful of people.

Why so many voluntary organizations? One explanation concerns the sociological hypothesis that the greater the level of economic development, the greater the number of voluntary organizations not governed by kinship criteria. I do not place much value on this explanation with regard to Olowo, for the fact that the family was suppressed makes it a very atypical case.

A second possibility has to do with the social structure of traditional Yoruba society. I have in mind an organization called the *egbe* society (Bascom, 1969, p. 48). This is an informal group of people who join together when young and maintain close ties for years, holding meetings and encouraging each other's advancement. The numerous voluntary associations in Olowo may be an extension of the *egbe* phenomenon.

The most promising explanation, however, concerns the need for intimacy. The several face-to-face groups may partly fill the vacuum created by suppression of the family. They permit sustained interaction at a personal level. Thus while the family substitutes provide members with an identity, the smaller groups may provide them with intimacy. Together they result in a high degree of solidarity for the entire village.

Finally, I want to raise again the problem of functional and structural indispensibility. I have said that while I assume the child-rearing and socialization functions must be fulfilled, I do not assume that specific concrete structures must exist to do so. A slightly different problem concerns teleology. The impression may have been given that the kindergarten and line, etc., came into existence in order to act as family substitutes. This was not my intention. These other structures could have existed even if the family had not been weakened; but since the family was suppressed, their functions expanded to fulfill these needs.

4. Discussion:
Impact of the Communal System

The purpose of the preceding chapters was to describe the manner in which the economy came to be organized along communal lines, and to indicate two consequences: the suppression of the family and the emergence of family substitutes. The purpose of this chapter is to consider two major problems. First, why did the changes in economic and family organization take place? Second, what is the significance of the Olowo case for the assumption that the family is universal?

I shall begin by breaking the first problem down into several specific problems. The initial one concerns the origin of the communal system. What model of communalism existed for the members of Olowo to copy? There is no satisfactory solution for this problem. Communalism on the scale practiced in Olowo is not found in Ilaje, in other parts of Nigeria, nor in West Africa in general.

Some evidence of collective behavior in the economic realm does exist in West Africa. For example, Ames (1963) describes the cooperative work groups among the Wolof of Gambia and Senegal, and Goody (1958) documents a comparable phenomenon in Ghana. Similar evidence also can be drawn from Nigeria. Communal work projects are prevalent among the Ibo, as well as contribution clubs which allow a person to participate in an investment with potential returns far beyond what an individual could normally realize (Ardener, 1953, and Ottenberg, 1963). Indeed, it is quite possible that the most important factor in the rapid industrialization of the Ibo prior to the civil war was not the intense individualism most authors stress, but rather their preparedness to act collectively.[1]

The Yoruba themselves are not devoid of collective economic activity. The *esusu* is a contribution club similar to that found among the Ibo.[2] And within both

---

[1] Both Ottenberg (1963, p. 137) and Uchendu (1965, p. 103) suggest that the high achievement drive among the Ibo is in terms not only of individual but also of group achievement. However, no investigator to my knowledge has yet taken up the theme of collective achievement among the Ibo and tried to relate it to their successful modernization. Indeed, the most thorough work on the subject, Levine's *Dreams and Deeds* (1966), does not entertain the collective factor at all.

[2] Little (1957, p. 584) refers to the *esusu* in his study of voluntary organizations. For a more thorough analysis see Bascom (1952).

Western and Eastern Nigeria cooperative farms have been established for several years. These of course are not necessarily an expression of indigenous communal behavior. But they do indicate that such models are not absent.

With respect to collective behavior contained within the traditional society itself, Schwab (1955, p. 357) shows that the Yoruba lineage has semicommunal functions:

Although work is not organized on a communal basis within a lineage, economic relationships and obligations in terms of exchange services and goods extend beyond the basic unit of production and consumption—father and sons—to the whole patrikin group. A lineage has a collective responsibility for the contribution of goods and services for the marriage and funeral ceremonies of its members. It shares in the execution of religious and ancestral ceremonies. It provides for the care of the elders and the indigent and performs mutual labor services during critical periods of the farming cycle, for the construction of a house or any other important task undertaken by any of its members.

Finally, within Ilaje itself some evidence of communal action can be found. For example, villages cooperate with each other to clear the shallow rivers and canals that lead to the larger waterways in the interior and thence to the mainland. Each village is usually assigned a section of the river to dredge.

It is clear, then, that communalism is not entirely alien to West Africa in general, to other parts of Nigeria, or even to Ilaje. This does not modify the original statement that the Olowo system is unique. The crucial factor concerns the range of communal behavior. The collective work gangs among the Wolof, the Lo Dagaba, the Ibo, and to a lesser degree the Ilaje, are hardly comparable to the Olowo case. They constitute a minute portion of economic activities. In Ilaje, for example, one may contribute less than half a dozen days in a year to such work. In contrast, work in large gangs or in the modified form of the departments represents almost all economic activity in Olowo.

Similarly, such phenomena as the contribution clubs do not modify the basic structure of the economy. Nor for that matter do the few days of communal work. People continue to be motivated in terms of an economic system that gives priority to self rather than collective orientation. The small degree of communal activity is an insignificant anomaly within the capitalist framework. The implication is that the decision to establish communalism in Olowo cannot be explained satisfactorily in terms of pre-existing models of the same behaviour.

What alternative explanations exist? The members of Olowo do not have to be prompted to provide one. As reported earlier, they stress that Olowo was not founded with the idea that it would become a "community." It was not until a year had passed that a decision to this effect was taken. The members contend that communalism was adopted then on religious grounds. By religion they mean two things. First, the prophets saw in visions that the village should be organized communally. Second, they wanted to follow in the steps of the early Christians.

The association of communalism and religion in this sense is very different from its association with the term "community" as described earlier. In the present sense religion is the independent variable; communalism is the result of religious goals. In the earlier sense religion was the dependent variable; as communalism began to occupy a central position in the value system, it took on a religious connotation.

My impression is that the communal system should not be explained as a consequence of religious beliefs. This stance rests partly upon an examination of several visions in Olowo. From this I concluded that visions are employed by the elite, perhaps unconsciously in most cases, as signs that their power is legitimate, and as means of supporting their policies. The vision of communalism may also be of this nature.

Nevertheless, the religious connection may be significant. It is difficult to imagine a group of uneducated fishermen gathering together and deciding that the most appropriate structure in order to industrialize was communalism. It is even more dubious that communalism could be imposed upon more than 1000 people if it only served economic ends. Both its initial introduction and successful implementation are more understandable if it does have a religious connotation. But this does not mean that religious beliefs inspired the Olowo people to adopt communalism. Instead the leaders of the village may have dressed it up in religious symbolism in order to make it more palatable to their followers.

This leads directly to the final explanation. It may be argued, as indeed do the members of Olowo, that the communal system was the idea of the first *oba*. Before having research experience, I was reluctant to reduce the level of explanation lower than the role. I still would argue that one must clearly recognize what constitutes the sociological perspective, and must exhaust this explanation before moving to a different level, such as the psychological. However, when one is trying to solve a specific problem in a concrete social unit (such as the introduction of communalism into Olowo) one can no longer respect professional boundaries.

My argument, then, is that the communal system can be traced mainly to one individual. But it is important to make a distinction between the introduction and the successful implementation of this innovation. The latter can be understood in both sociological and psychological terms. From the sociological point of view, it was said earlier that Olowo has a highly centralized authority structure, with the *oba* occupying the most important position. His power was enhanced and symbolized by the fact that he was called *oba,* a term of authority taken from traditional Yoruba society. It also was fostered by the fact that Olowo grew out of a religious movement. The first *oba* was considered to be the greatest prophet in the village. The implication is clear: significant power is intrinsic to the role of the Olowo leader. Such power would help him to impose the communal system on his people.

The psychological dimension is also important. The first *oba* is said to have been an energetic, brilliant, awesome personality. Few of his flock dared speak to him, and he did not hesitate to personally flog members of the elite if they failed to obey him. The implication is that while the role of *oba* itself contains great power, the first leader exhausted the role of all that it had to offer. This means that the successful adoption of the communal system is at least partly related to the personal qualities of the first *oba*.

I now turn to the *introduction* of the communal system. It was argued that no comparable model was available for the villagers to copy. Can it be understood in terms of the personality of the first *oba?* I shall argue that it cannot, and that any attempt to do so is to result in a deceptive explanation. For how did he arrive at the idea? He had no more experience of similar models of social organization than had his subjects. The implication is that the idea of a communal society was a random element in one person's consciousness that somehow materialized at this time and place. The problem of the origin of communalism in Olowo has not been resolved by reference to the *oba*'s personality. It merely has been restated at a different level of abstraction.

A further problem concerns the origin of family suppression. In Chapter 2 it was argued that communalism in Olowo is primarily an economic phenomenon, and that the suppression of the family is a consequence of changes in economic organization. Some support for this argument was provided by reference to attitudes: the goals of the village are economic, not familial; communalism is a means of realizing the economic goals. Given the manner in which the family was weakened, it now is possible to reinforce this argument by reference to social structure.

I said earlier that the changes in the economy and the family both began in 1948. However, the range of change that occurred then is very different for the two structures. With the exception of the gradual emergence of the department as a major unit of organization, the communalization of the economy was completed in 1948. In contrast, the only major change in family organization in 1948 was the distribution of women among those who did not have a wife. Other changes such as the separation of the village into male and female sectors, the distribution of children among adults other than their own parents, and the founding of the kindergarten, did not occur until several years later. Furthermore, the emergence of family substitutes such as the line and line leader came later still. The implication is clear: both from a perspective of attitudes and social structure, the changes in the family seem to have followed those in the economy.

A further question arises: why should the communal system have led to the suppression of the family? I can answer this question more satisfactorily by first confronting a different problem: the manner in which the communal system and the suppression of the family contributed to the growth of the economy.

The communal system has two main advantages. It makes available large labor units that can be manipulated by the leaders of the village as they wish. For example, hundreds of men and women have worked together building canals, roads, houses and boats. This work was achieved quickly and efficiently. The communal system also makes large sums of capital available. The members of Olowo worked without wages, and the profits from the numerous industries were fed back into the economy. Both the large labor units and the available capital contributed to the numerous economic innovations in Olowo and hence to its rapid development.

The family, in turn, contributed to the development of Olowo by virtue of its *lack* of influence on the economy. My argument is that the communal system and the family are rival phenomena. Both compete as a primary principle of social organization. The stronger the family, the less likely the success of the communal system, and thus the less likely economic development.

A similar argument has been made by William Goode. As he states (1966, p. 248), "Rapid industrialization . . . would . . . require family ties to be reduced as much as possible." Goode said this applies not only to the extended family but to the nuclear family as well. He also remarks (p. 248) that ". . . some variant of a 'communal family' pattern would answer the demands of industrialism better than a conjugal family could. Plato's variant was more radical than the Chinese blueprint; but in both, as in the kibbutz, the goal is to weaken kinship obligations, whether between parent and child or between spouses." This is precisely what occurred in Olowo. Thus the suppression of the family in order to give greater prominence to communalism was a positive factor for Olowo's rapid development.

A final problem remains. Let us assume that the family *was* weakened in order to promote communalism. Even if this is correct, how explicitly was the incompatibility of the communal system with a strong family recognized by Olowo people?

I have stressed that no adequate explanation can be found of why communalism was adopted. Given the communal system, however, the suppression of the family is easier to explain. The sociological conditions for the changes in family organization were present in the village. For this reason it is not as necessary to reduce the explanation to the psychological level. At the same time it is likely that the negative relationship between communalism and the family was not recognized by most members. My suspicion is that it was the first *oba* who saw most clearly what had to be done.

Is the Family Universal? Olowo and the Kibbutz Compared

The other major problem will now be considered: the significance of the Olowo case for the assumption that the family is universal. Most social scientists appear to accept this assumption. Even Levy (1952, p. 205), who observes that there is no logical reason to suppose the family is a concrete structural requisite of every society, speculates that it probably is a requisite nevertheless.

The most thorough study to establish the universality of the family has been done by Murdock. Generalizing from a cross-cultural survey of 250 societies, he concludes that both marriage and one type of family organization—the nuclear variety—are universal. Murdock's conclusions have been challenged by Spiro, who argues that if Murdock's definitions of marriage and the family are accepted, neither structure exists in the kibbutz. As will be shown, Olowo diverges from the criteria of marriage and the family in much the same manner as does the kibbutz. The Olowo material thus has special significance: it reinforces Spiro.

Let us first consider marriage. Murdock states that marriage is a social institution that combines two cultural patterns: a sexual relationship and economic cooperation between at least two persons of the opposite sex. In his words (1966, p. 8): "Sexual unions without economic cooperation are common and there are relationships between men and women involving a division of labor without sexual gratification, e.g., between brother and sister, master and maidservant, or employer and secretary, but marriage exists only when the economic and the sexual are united into one relationship, and this combination occurs only in marriage. Marriage, thus defined, is found in every known human society."

As Spiro shows, however, in the kibbutz there is neither economic cooperation nor a division of labor between couples of the opposite sex. A division of labor does exist according to sex. However, a man and a woman do not constitute an economic unit. Instead, the community is the basic economic unit for each of them. The Olowo case is similar to the kibbutz. Sex is a major principle of the division of labor. For example, men catch the fish and women process it. Husband and wife do not constitute an economic unit, however. As in the kibbutz each member works for the community—or more specifically for the department.

It should be added that in both the kibbutz and Olowo there is an ideal of sexual equality in the occupational realm. In the kibbutz the ideal is not attained. As Spiro points out, there is a tendency for the men to take part in "productive" work, and the women to take part in "service" work: cooking, cleaning, caring for children, etc. In Olowo the ideal translates empirically into a tendency for women to perform the same hard physical work that men do, such as cementing roads. But it does not translate into equality of opportunity.

Spiro shows that the kibbutz also is exceptional with respect to sexual union. Marriage itself does not require any formality. Sexual activity is legitimate without marriage. When a couple fall in love, they are given a joint room of their own. When they fall out of love, they return to separate rooms. Only when a woman becomes pregnant is a formal marriage bond introduced. This is necessary because in Israel illegitimate children have no civil rights.

Again Olowo coincides with the kibbutz. Marriage was banned entirely at two different periods. Even when marriage existed, husband and wife did not live together. The implication is that both Olowo and the kibbutz are exceptions to Murdock's assumption of the universality of marriage.

I now turn to the family, which Murdock (1966, p. 1) defines as ". . . a social group characterized by common residence, economic cooperation, and reproduction. It includes adults of both sexes, at least two of whom maintain a socially approved sexual relationship, and one or more children, own or adopted, of the sexually cohabiting adults."

As indicated earlier, Murdock argues that the nuclear family is a universal human social grouping. Moreover, it always performs four vital functions: the sexual, the economic, the reproductive, and the educational. Murdock states that agencies or institutions outside the family may contribute to the fulfillment of these functions, but never to the extent of supplanting the family.

In considering these criteria, Spiro remarks that it is even more difficult to identify the family in the kibbutz than to identify marriage. As he points out, the kibbutz family does include two adults of the opposite sex who maintain a legitimate sexual relationship, and their children. But it does not include common residence (since children live in dormitories), or economic cooperation (at least not between spouses). Nor does it include the education and socialization function, since this is undertaken by nurses and teachers in communal dormitories. Spiro concludes that following Murdock's definition, the family does not exist in the kibbutz.

Olowo diverges from the criteria of the family laid down by Murdock in much the same way as does the kibbutz. The Olowo family is not characterized by economic cooperation or common residence. Nor does it have the main responsibility for socialization of children. Finally, both the sexual and reproductive functions have for brief periods been performed outside the family.

Most of these generalizations have already been illustrated. As was shown, there is a division of labor according to sex, but it is functional at the community level, not between husband and wife. As to residence, it has been shown that Olowo is split into male and female sectors and that children do not generally live with either parent of the same sex after the age of five or six. In Chapter 2 we saw that the socialization function is mainly provided by family substitutes. Finally, both the sexual and reproductive functions have occurred outside the family. This took place when marriage was banned.

To conclude, Spiro challenges the assumptions of Murdock with regard to the universality of both marriage and family. The Olowo case supports Spiro's position. This is significant, for by itself one case may not be so crucial. Given two cases, the criticisms against Murdock must be taken more seriously.

It would be unfortunate to leave the discussion as it now stands, because the relevancy of the kibbutz and Olowo for Murdock's work is limited in at least four ways. The first concerns a distinction that Spiro makes between the structural-functional and psychological perspectives. He argues that in a structural sense the family does not exist in the kibbutz, but in a psychological sense it does. As he points out, even though parents and their children do not live together, there are strong emotional bonds between them. These operate to such an extent that family members constitute "a distinct and recognizable social group." (1963, p. 123).

If the time element is specified, the Olowo family also can be said to exist in a psychological sense. After the third *oba* assumed office the family became stronger both in a structural-functional sense and a psychological sense. Not only did relatives begin to live together, but the members of the village began to conceptualize their social universe in terms of their family connections. The concepts of kinship identification and kinship consciousness were introduced in order to express the emerging psychological reality of the family—a reality which outpaced the structural changes in the family.

Quite apart from the psychological dimension, a second limitation is that the family was never completely demolished in either the kibbutz or Olowo. As regards the kibbutz, Talmon-Garber (1962, p. 471), Irvine (1952, p. 247), and Mogey (1962, p. 412) emphasize this point. With respect to Olowo, in Chapter 1 it was shown that the members of the village were wrong to say the family did not exist. People knew the identity of their relatives, a form of marriage was present most of the time, and a proportion of close relatives of the same sex lived together. While neither the kibbutz nor Olowo meet Murdock's criteria of the family and marriage, then, this does not mean that all behavior that would be classified as belonging to the family and marriage is absent.

This leads directly to a third limitation of the material: the problem of interpretation. As Spiro himself observes (1963, p. 123), there are at least two alternatives open to him. One is to conclude that marriage and the family do not exist in the kibbutz, which is the interpretation he adopts. The other is to modify Murdock's definitions of marriage and the family. The second alternative appears to be preferable. To do otherwise is to treat definitions not as tentative and heuristic devices, but as rigid categories. The danger of this is aptly demonstrated in the cases of both Olowo and kubbutzim, for by following Murdock too faithfully there is a tendency to ignore the limited amount of family behavior that does exist.

Levy and Fallers (1959) challenge Murdock's conclusion that the nuclear family is universal and always performs four functions. They observe that comparative political analysis stagnated until an analytic concept of the political was introduced. Their argument is that there will be little advancement in cross-cultural studies of the family until an analytic rather than substantive definition is established.

In an article entitled "Is the Family Universal?" (1954) Spiro arrives at the same conclusion as in his major work. From a structural point of view the family in the kibbutz does not exist. But Spiro refers to the tendency of the kibbutz as a whole to act as a large extended family, and supports his argument by indicating that all members of the kibbutz he studied married outsiders. This in spite of the fact that there are no rules of exogamy. While the same tendency of identification with the community is found in Olowo, endogamous marriage is the rule rather than the exception.

Spiro's article was published in 1954. In an appendix written four years later, and published in 1960 (Bell and Vogel, 1960), he questions his earlier position. Like Levy and Fallers, he suggests that an analytic definition of the family and marriage is necessary. In his words, " . . . cross-cultural research is most fruitfully advanced by means of analytic, rather than substantive or enumerative definitions. Thus, for example, we might want to define marriage as 'any socially sanctioned relationship between consanguineally-related cohabitating adults of opposite sex which satisfied felt needs—mutual, symmetrical, or complementary.' A non-enumerative definition of this type would certainly embrace all known cases now termed 'marriage' and would, at the same time, include the kibbutz case as well." (1960, pp. 73–74)

Just as Spiro finds Murdock's definition too narrow, Spiro's definition would be too narrow to handle cases such as fictive marriage, in which a woman marries another woman, or cases such as group marriage suggested by Gough (1959) in her work on the Nayars. What is important, however, is that Spiro is less prepared now to say that marriage and the family do not exist in the kibbutz. He prefers instead to change Murdock's definition in order that the kibbutz can be accommodated.

My own inclination is to resist the attempt to erect a definition of marriage and the family that includes every case. To do so is to make it so general that it is insensitive to even the most gross variation. If anthropologists do feel it is necessary to formulate a concept that is universally applicable, I would suggest that they also form a less general concept—one that is intended for the majority of known marriage and family types. Cases such as the kibbutz and Olowo then can be treated as interesting exceptions to the general phenomenon.

The fourth limitation of the material is that Olowo and the kibbutz are only small communities, not whole societies. How legitimate is it then to conclude that they challenge Murdock's conclusions? Part of the difficulty in answering this question is that Murdock does not seem to have restricted the level of generality of his work to large-scale societies. But if we make this restriction for him, the significance of Olowo and the kibbutz is diminished.

Spiro has flirted with this possible limitation of his material. One of his conclusions is that the kibbutz can function without a family because it functions as a family itself. But this is only likely to happen, he states (Spiro, 1954, p. 846), in a society small enough in order that members can perceive themselves psychologically as kin.

In concluding, I raise the question of why the family was weakened in the kibbutz. This may shed further light on this problem in Olowo. Spiro stresses two factors, both of which concern equality. First, an attempt was made to eliminate the "patriarchal" father, and thus the subjection of wife and children (Spiro, 1963, p. 121. See also Talmon-Garber, 1962, p. 471). No such reason exists in Olowo. It was not the father that was being eliminated, but the entire extended family. This was not done because of the authoritarian relation of the father to the wife and children. Instead it was done in order to foster the communal system and hence economic development. As evidence, women and youth still must demonstrate their obedience to the men by terms of salutation and by genuflecting before them.

Second, an attempt was made to eradicate the traditional dependence of women on men. This goal was a product of a strong feminist movement in the kibbutz (Spiro, 1963, p. 122). Again no such reason exists in Olowo. Women in Ilaje are dominated by the men. In Olowo it is the same. In spite of the rapid industrialization of the village, the supposed superiority of the men has not diminished. In sum, the suppression of the family in Olowo cannot be understood in terms of either father domination or female inequality. Instead it is related to the efforts to industrialize by virtue of communalism.

Talmon (1965, p. 262) suggests additional reasons for the weakening of the family in the kibbutz. The demographic characteristics, in which many young people had no family of their own, and the fact that the kibbutzim were training centres for the youth movements, reinforced the need for a community rather than a family orientation. Talmon also remarks that the kibbutzim had semimilitary functions, which were facilitated by the communal rather than family orientation. The demographic factor is also significant in Olowo, for it seems that many of the charter members in 1947 left part or all of their immediate families in the nearby villages. As regards the military function, Olowo people say that one reason they adopted the communal system was in order to be united against the attacks of their hostile neighbours.

Finally, neither the kibbutz nor Olowo has stood still. In the kibbutz in the past there was no legal marriage until the woman became pregnant, and spouses rarely interacted publicly. In Olowo in the past husband and wife did not live together and social activities based upon family ties were prohibited.

All this is changing. Couples in the kibbutz now address each other with the terms "husband" and "wife", which was unheard of in the past; further, family outings are becoming common. In Olowo, husband and wife and offspring are beginning to live together; and the family is becoming a major principle of social organization. Both communities may be said to be undergoing a process of normalization. This process, as it will be shown in Part II, is not limited to the family. It impinges upon other structures such as the economy.

Part Two

CAPITALISM AND THE EMERGENCE OF THE FAMILY

---

5. The Capitalist System

The communal system which was introduced in Olowo in 1948 persisted through the reigns of the first and second *obas*. But after the present *oba* assumed office in 1966 a major change took place: private enterprise emerged on a small scale.[1] The purpose of this chapter is to describe the precise manner in which the change took place, to indicate the range of private enterprise in Olowo in 1970, and to consider some of the consequences of the change for the community. No attempt will be made now to explain why the structure of the economy was modified, or to show how it is related to the major change described in the next chapter—the emergence of the family as a legitimate institution. These will be dealt with in Chapter 7.

The main index of the transformation of the economy is that members are now allowed to have a personal income. It will be remembered that a few years after Olowo was founded three distinct patterns of work emerged. These were work in departments, communal labor, and individual labor. What happened was that the system of rewards relating to two of these organizational types was modified. First, *all* profits from individual labor are now retained by the workers. However, there is not a direct correlation between individual effort and personal wealth. This is because *some* profits from departmental work are now shared by members of each department. This second source of income is greater than the first, and the amount is determined by the collective achievements of the entire department, rather than by the contribution of the individual.

There are two types of individual labor: legitimate and semilegitimate. Legitimate work in turn is conducted both on a part-time and full-time basis. One example of part-time individual work concerns people who go to the seashore early in the morning before their regular job in the department begins. The men wade into the water with their nets and catch the fish. The women usually assume the responsibility for processing and marketing the catch, which is dried or smoked and sold in the Olowo market or in markets further away. Previously the profits of this work were turned over to the community. Now all profits are kept by the individual.

A second example again is connected with the fishing industry. In the past three

---

[1] I have described this innovation elsewhere (Barrett, 1972).

years a few members have begun to build fishponds. This is done by digging a hole approximately 20 feet square. The hole must be boarded off in order that the fish will not escape during the floods of the wet season. It must also be deep enough so that it will not evaporate in the dry season. After the pond is constructed it is stocked with tarpon about two inches long that are caught in the fresh-water rivers. If left in the rivers they make their way to the sea after reaching a certain stage of maturity. The tarpon are fed small fish caught by net and spear. Eventually they grow to about two or three feet in length. They are delicious to eat, and can be sold for 15 or more shillings each.

These types of individual labor are not new to the community. However in the past they were not a focus of individual competition, nor were they pursued with the same intensity. This is especially the case with the fishponds. A few years ago a similar pond was built for the first *oba*. However, the fish did not thrive, and the pond was soon discarded. In contrast, almost 30 ponds have been constructed since 1966. The reason is that they are a source of private income for the individual.

Most individual labor is carried out on a part-time basis. While the following example of such work that is full-time is not typical, it is included because it indicates clearly the transformed structure of the economy. The case involves the community photographer. He has performed this function for several years. When he first began, the community gave him what funds were required to purchase equipment. The community no longer provides this service. For example, in 1968 the photographer decided he needed equipment for enlarging, as well as new cameras. The cost of the equipment was approximately 180 pounds. Instead of supplying the photographer with this amount the community decided to lend him 100 pounds. The photographer had charged members for photographs for the previous two years, and had saved 60 pounds. He waited until he had earned the remaining 20 pounds and then purchased the new equipment. The photographer's work is good, and the members constantly require his services. He expected to pay the 100 pounds back to the community by the end of 1970.

A form of labor among individuals that is only semi-legitimate is what the community calls "business." As an example, if a man wants to purchase a desk from the carpentry department he may be asked to pay 10 pounds. Instead of agreeing to do so, he may approach one of the carpenters and ask him to do the work privately at a reduced cost. In one such case a member agreed to build a desk for a resident of a neighboring village. He did the work in an empty building at night. When the desk was completed it was sent by canoe to the outsider under cover of darkness and sold for 5 pounds.

A further example involves the tailoring department. Rather than paying the standard full price for a garment it is easy to persuade one of the tailors to do the work after hours. The buyer is happy because the price is reduced. The tailor is pleased because the profits are his own. This is what is termed "business." It also is called "dodging." When put in the context of the communal system, it would seem to be an illegitimate form of behavior. However, the new *oba* is reported to be in favor of it, interpreting it as another source of economic competition that is healthy for the village. It should be stressed that business is not new in Olowo, but with the introduction of private enterprise it has achieved some degree of legitimacy.

The second major type of labor occurs at the level of groups, is carried out entirely on a full-time basis, and takes place within the structure of the department. Previously members did not receive any direct payment for this work. Now it results in two types of monetary reward. First, while they still are not allowed to retain the profits of the department, when the money is handed over to the community treasury at the end of each month the manager will now keep out a few pounds to distribute among the workers. The amount received varies according to the post of the worker. The manager, for example, receives two or three pounds more than the others. This monthly source of income may be termed a "dash."

Second, while the members of each department do not receive a salary, a form of payment has been introduced called a "bonus," which each member receives one to three times a year, depending upon the department. The members are concerned to explain that the bonus is not a salary. They do this in order to maintain the appearance of communalism in Olowo.

A further example of the new reward system is again related to the various departments. Before 1966 there was only one store in the village where small items could be obtained. This was called the Olowo Community Shop. In the last three years six other shops have been opened, each of which is owned by one of the departments. All the shops carry an identical range of stock. Given a communal society in which internal competition is supposedly foreign, this overlap is not rational. In effect, the several new shops are indices of the transformation of the economy of Olowo, and in particular of departmental competition. For example, both the bread department and the tailoring department own a shop. When a person goes to collect bread he is enticed into making a further purchase at the departmental shop. The same occurs in the tailoring department. Before 1967 no money was charged in the original shop. Now in all the shops, including the original one, members must pay for what they buy.

A final example of group labor concerns the fishing industry. The catch from the trawlers is carried in carts to a specific building where it is dumped on the floor. The task of separating the fish according to type belongs to the women, whose reward consists of a pile of the culled fish. The amount they receive varies according to their age: the older the woman, the larger the pile. After the catch is separated it is weighed and sold to customers. These are mainly Olowo women. Since 1967 they have not been allowed to collect the fish free, but must pay for it. The women take the fish away, dry it, and in turn sell it in the market.

In spite of the fact that the women pay for the fish, their profits are still immense. A pile that they purchase for 1 pound may bring in a return of 1 pound and 10 shillings or more after it has been dried. It is unreasonable to suppose they keep all the profits, and in fact they do not. Each month the accumulated profits are turned over to the community. It may be suspected that the women will attempt to "dodge." However, their work is organized in such a way as to reduce "business" to a minimum. No woman works alone. Instead, all work in groups of four or five. Each group has a leader who is a trusted member. It is her responsibility to make certain all profits from the group go to the community at the end of each month.

The system of reward is identical to that in other departments. At the end of the month the group leader retains a few pounds cash and distributes it among her mates, and the community provides each group of women with a bonus. The size of the bonus varies according to the output of the group. As in the case of the other departments the basic system of reward is indirect. Furthermore, it is not the individual who is rewarded, but the group as a whole.

Group labor, then, is more dominant than individual labor. It is carried out entirely on a full-time basis. Its rewards are primarily indirect. And the size of the reward varies according to the output of the entire group, rather than to individual productivity within the group.

One further type of reward warrants attention. As part of the community's ideology of modernity, indigenous ceremonies and rituals are rejected as time-wasting and evil. However, they do celebrate the end of each year with countless parties and one major ceremony. At that time work comes to a stop, and members conducting community business at points throughout Nigeria are summoned home. It may be speculated that the year-end ceremony fills a necessary social gap in the community, given the absence of traditional rituals. However, this interpretation suffers a little too much from functional indispensibility. Irrespective of its ritual significance, the ceremony has an important practical function. It is then that rewards are distributed for outstanding performance.

Consonant with previous descriptions, such rewards are both immaterial and material, both individually and collectively determined. The epitome of immaterial reward is an appointment to the prestigious Council of the Elders. Material rewards include clothing, bicycles, and motorcycles. These are donated both to individuals and to corporate groups. In the first case a particularly industrious member may be given a bicycle. In the second case a department that has greatly exceeded its estimated productivity may benefit from a department that has not done so well. For example, if the carpenters have worked hard, and the tailors not so hard, the latter department may be ordered by the *oba* to give a shirt to every member of the carpentry department.

In summary, there are now several sources of personal income in the community. First, money can be gained by individual initiative outside one's regular occupation. This includes both legitimate and semi-legitimate work. Second, one can gain money from one's regular occupation in a department. This includes both the monthly dash and the thrice annual bonus. Third, one can be rewarded at the year-end ceremony.

The oba's *palace in Olowo, resting upon ground built up above the water line.*

Part of the oba's *new palace, under construction in 1972.*

The Mixed Economy

Although private enterprise has been introduced into Olowo, the changes in the economy have been limited. By retaining the structure of the departments, and the consequent system of rewards in terms of collective rather than individual achievement, the development of private enterprise has been inhibited. As a result the present economic structure represents a mixture of capitalist and communal systems.

One index of this mixture is that while individuals are now allowed to keep private money, its size relative to the collective profits of the village is very small. Indeed, community policy allows members to retain only 7% of all profits. The remaining 93% is claimed by the village treasury.[2]

Since such a high percentage is claimed by the community, it may be thought that the incentive of the private purse would be nullified. It may also be assumed that many, perhaps the majority, of people would attempt to "dodge." With respect to incentive it must be realized that in the past no private income could be retained. Thus even a small personal income now is valued; and, in comparison with the average income of neighbouring villagers, 7% of the collective profits in Olowo is still a significant amount.

Relative to "dodging" it must be remembered that most work occurs in the departments. This labor is well-organized. It is not difficult to assure that the stipulated 93% of the profits are delivered to the community. In cases where supervision is more difficult, steps have been taken to make certain the profits are not kept by individuals. The system of control with respect to the women who sell fish has already been described: they all work in small groups. Further, the income derived from individual part-time work, such as catching fish at the seashore in the early morning, or conducting "business," is in fact quite small. The community treasury does not suffer by allowing members to keep it. Indirectly, then, the private purse benefits the community as much as the individual. By permitting it, the community fosters the incentive of individual reward. By restricting its size, the community avoids jeopardizing its own treasury.

A second policy reflecting the mix in the economy has to do with what one member called "the circulation of profits." This is an ingenious method in which the recent novelty of the private purse again ultimately enriches the communal purse. A restriction is placed on how one's private money is spent. No goods should be purchased outside the village. Since basic necessities such as bread, clothing, and shoes, as well as minor items from combs to brassieres, are available in the community, the objective is to a great extent realized.

---

[2]This figure was provided by the *oba*. From other sources I was told that members are allowed to retain one shilling and sixpence on the pound, which works out to approximately 7%.

The advantage of this system to the community can readily be explained. Radios, rubber boots, yams, etc., are all bought in bulk from outside the village. This constitutes a significant reduction in price. Furthermore, those in charge of purchasing such goods know the exact price; in a society where bargaining is a normal procedure, the advantage held by the expert again reduces the cost of the item. This factor is especially relevant in Olowo. Because until recently people did not pay money for goods received, they often did not know their value, and were easily cheated outside the community. This was particularly the case with the younger members who were born in Olowo and knew no other system than their own brand of communalism.

These are not the most important advantages. Consider the following process: when a member decides to buy a lamp or a flashlight, he makes the purchase in one of the community shops, or departments. Now this means that the profit of the sale remains in the village. It is not lost to the outside world. Further, most of the profit gradually ends up in the community treasury. This is because departments only retain a portion of what they earn.

It is not only individual members who are encouraged to make their purchases in Olowo. When possible the various departments buy goods from each other. For example, if the shoe department requires nails it should buy these from the carpentry department. In order to encourage members and departments to spend their money in Olowo, some departments are allowed to supplement their stock with goods obtained from Lagos or elsewhere. For example, in addition to the shoes made by the community, one can purchase Bata models at the showroom; and a stock of shirts and trousers purchased from Lagos is carried by the tailoring department.

The shoe department increases the prices of the Bata shoes by three or four shillings. The tailoring department makes a similar profit on its imported stock. The size of the profit from such sales is not unlimited. If each department were permitted to charge what it wished, people would be reluctant to make their purchases in the community. In order to avert this danger the *oba* has decreed that profits from the sale of expensive goods must not exceed 10%, and from petty items must not be greater than 15%. According to the members this order is frequently ignored.

In effect, central to the system of "the circulation of profits" is the perpetual flow of capital. Members are not encouraged to hoard their money. It should be spent, but only in Olowo. There is some exchange of cash among individuals, as, for example, when one person buys a chicken or a fish from another. Most purchases, however, are made from the various departments, or from the shops belonging to them. The major flow of capital, then, is from individuals to departments and among departments themselves. In both cases the bulk of the capital eventually is claimed by the community treasurer. Thus each time a transaction is made, whether between an individual and a department, or between departments themselves, the community purse is replenished.

A final example of the retention of some degree of communal social organization involves communal labor. It still occurs on an average of twice a week in the dry season. When the town crier rings his bell and announces a specific project to be done, all members are expected to respond. Usually about two or three hundred men appear at the designated spot, and perhaps 25 or 35 women. This work does not bring in any direct material reward. However, its importance both for the work achieved and for the individuals contributing is significant. Large-scale projects requiring hundreds of men still can be done quickly in Olowo. Further, communal work is symbolic of the values that have for long been dominant in the village. This means that an individual's contribution is a moral contribution. It is for this reason that no ambitious member can afford to miss communal labor. Thus whenever the bell is rung to summon members to cut grass or clear logs from the canal, there is an over-representation of both established and aspiring members of the elite.

Thus far, the restrictions imposed upon private enterprise have been considered at the general level of action of the social system. These restrictions of course impinge upon the individual actor, as the following cases reveal. It will be recalled that since the economy was modified six new shops sprang up, all of which charge for the items they carry. During the Christmas celebrations the manager of one of the shops decided to open a bar in the back room. Because of his position, it was legitimate for him to travel to Lagos regularly to purchase stock. On these trips he began to bring back beer, and he bought a record player. The word was passed among the young people that at 10 P.M. every night they could listen to music, drink beer, and dance in the shop. Those who responded were mostly unmarried men and married women; since most girls marry shortly after puberty there was no supply of single women.

For almost two weeks the bar was kept a secret. But then husbands began to ask where their wives were. More important, the existing institution that legitimately provided the function of entertainment complained that it had no customers. This was the community hotel. Inevitably the secret bar was discovered, and immediately closed down. The manager's record player was seized, and his behavior was condemned by the village leaders.

A second case concerns a young man in the village who had recently purchased a radio worth about 20 pounds. He was aware that he would be considered too junior to have such a possession. For this reason he told all who inquired that the radio belonged to a more important member. The story was soon uncovered, and the young man was summoned by the deputy *oba* to explain how he managed to purchase the radio. In spite of his explanation that he had saved almost every penny of the money accumulated from private fishing in the sea, from the dash, and the bonus, the radio was taken from him.

This case reveals an important feature of the community at present. While people are now allowed to have private money, there is much ambiguity as regards the appropriate amount. This is especially true for low-status people, who are not expected to acquire the amenities enjoyed by the elite, such as radios. Regardless of a person's status, if the money he accumulates exceeds 20 pounds or so, he is expected to donate it to the community treasury. There is no mechanism to assure that this is done, and most people probably keep what they earn from private work. A possible exception concerns members in trouble. While I only have reliable data for one case, there seems to be a tendency for those in trouble to donate their private income to the community. The phenomenon, thus, is a means of retribution.

A last example of restricted enterprise concerns the outlets in the village for petty goods. In addition to the six new shops, a further change was that women were allowed to set up tiny stalls on the main boardwalk. At first the range of items sold was small: mostly soap, sardines, and margarine. After a few months both the number of stalls and the range of goods sold in them increased quickly, so that they began to offer competition to the shops. But the stalls, too, were subjected to the same restrictions as other economic activities. The *oba* said he did not like the owners of the stalls to hawk their goods all around the village, as is done in Yorubaland in general. Instead they had to keep their goods in one place, and not try to pull customers off the boardwalk. The stall owners have partly circumvented this decree. They often send their small children around the village with a container of the goods balanced on their heads. The pretence is that the children are taking the goods to some specific location. In reality they walk back and forth, marketing them in this way.

Consequences

Attention will now be directed to some of the consequences of the introduction of private enterprise. One consequence is that the range of amenities provided by the village has decreased. Bread, for example, previously was distributed free to every member. After the economy was modified, free bread was made available every morning at the line "hotel," a small building where residents of each line gathered to eat. If a person wanted bread at another time it was necessary to pay for it. By 1970 the system had changed once again: bread was not free at any time. As a result most of the women who owned the small stalls began to sell bread as well, making a slight profit after buying it at the bakery.

A further example concerns housing. All houses in the past were provided without charge, and in theory the practice continues. However, the community now is responsible only for part of the construction. Community carpenters will drive stilts into the mud and erect the framework. The individuals who intend to occupy the house are expected to complete it. Wood is provided without charge, but it is often difficult to obtain what is needed from the sawmill. In order to increase their chances, the prospective residents may invite the manager of the sawmill for entertainment. In the end, many people buy what they need from Lagos because of the frustration.

Small items such as light bulbs now must be paid for by the occupant. Paint is supposed to be free, but again there are obstacles to obtaining it. The landlord must get the consent of the manager of his department; if granted, the department will purchase the paint from the shop that stocks it. Departments are reluctant to finance such projects. As a result the landlord and the other residents usually contribute to a fund and buy their own paint.

A last example of the decrease in goods and services provided for the members concerns education. Olowo has its own primary and secondary schools. Fees are still free, but the guardian and kinsmen of students are now responsible for buying many of the required books. Furthermore, the community has decided not to provide school uniforms any longer. Instead each student must purchase his own.

A second important consequence of the changed economy is that individual expression is now allowed. For example, formerly everybody had to eat what was bought by the community. Rarely did the diet vary. Now members can use their own pocket money to buy tinned beans, eggs, etc. A further example is that it is now legitimate to construct the interior of one's house as one wishes. However, as we saw with respect to the amount of money and type of goods that are allowed, there are restrictions against exercising one's individual taste. For example, if a person consistently spends his money on food of his choice and fails to join the others in the special eating house, criticism is bound to follow. In one such case a man was condemned for his preference to eat by himself what his wife cooked. The same restrictions apply with housing. As indicated, the landlord is now free to construct the inside of his house as he likes. He can have three rooms or four or five. He can have a tablecloth, or cheap oilcloth for the floor if he wishes. But the *oba* insists that the outside of the houses must remain uniform throughout the village.

A final consequence of the change in the economy concerns stratification. Since the founding of the community the ideal of equality has been central to the value system. Equality in the past referred primarily to material objects, rather than to power and prestige. Most members had a similar standard of living, but a small elite ruled the community and enjoyed high status for doing so. It was my impression that since the introduction of private enterprise there had been a tendency for material reward to correspond more closely to a person's power and prestige. For example, the *oba* recently decided that large, two-story houses would be built for the managers of departments.

In order to develop this assumption, the three status categories employed for Tables 1.1 and 1.2 were used again. Each person was surveyed in order to see if he possessed a radio, record player, bicycle, or motorcycle. The results showed that the higher his status, the more likely he was to possess these objects. For example, all the high-status people and three-quarters of the upper-middle status people own a radio, but only half of the low-status people have one.

The results also revealed clear differences in the possession of these objects before and after the change in structure of the economy. The lower a person's status, the more likely it was that he had acquired them after 1966. For example, all of the high status people had a radio before 1966, but none of the upper-middle or low-status people had one then.

It was also found that there were two distinct methods of obtaining material goods since 1966: gifts from the *oba* and purchases with a person's own private money. Moreover, the higher a person's status, the more likely it is that he will receive a gift from the *oba*. For example, the majority of the upper-middle status people who have a radio received it as a gift from the *oba*, whereas the majority of those of low status with a radio bought it with the money they saved from the bonus, the dash, and private business.

This indicates that the *oba* continues to manipulate the reward system to a considerable degree. Yet low-status people now have the potential for purchasing objects formerly restricted to the elite. The implication is that by virtue of individual initiative low-status people can now move up the status ladder. However, as reflected in the case in which the radio was taken from the young man, there is a norm in the village that low-status people should not have valued objects. Further evidence of this is the fact that three-quarters of the upper-status and one-quarter of the upper-middle status people have a record player, but not one person of low status has one. This is not entirely because they lack money to buy the item. Instead they are discouraged from doing so because it is above their station.

6. The Emergence of the Family

The dominant fact about the family during the reigns of the first and second *obas* was the degree to which it was suppressed. The dominant fact since the third *oba* came to the throne is the degree to which the family has emerged as a viable and legitimate institution. As before, I will not try to explain now why the change occurred, or how it is related to the introduction of private enterprise. This will be done in Chapter 7.

Marriage

Two major changes in marital arrangements took place after the third *oba* assumed office. First, a formal marital bond was reestablished; this was accompanied by a high divorce rate. Second, polygyny was introduced. Each of these will be considered in some detail.

When the third *oba* came to the throne in 1966 he immediately reversed the policy of his predecessor and ordered all adults to take a partner. One informant stated that nobody was allowed to choose the same mate possessed before the second *oba* had banned marriage in 1963. Other informants disagreed. They said people were at liberty to choose as they wished. However, they did agree that only rarely did former partners select each other. This resulted in an exceptionally high divorce rate.

The term divorce is not quite precise. A general reason is that the discarding of one partner in Olowo was almost always accompanied by the acquisition of another (except when marriage was banned altogether). As Lloyd (1968) points out, this is the normal divorce procedure among the Yoruba. A second reason is specific to this particular situation: all marriage ties had been banned for three years. Divorce, then, refers to whether or not a person chose the partner he had before the reign of the second *oba*. If not, I classify it as a case of divorce.

In a sample of 14 houses in the male sector, in which 31 of the 53 residents were married, 21 of the 31 men have been divorced since Olowo was founded. In a sample of 10 houses in the female sector, in which 27 of the 40 residents were married, 20 of the 27 women have been divorced since the founding of Olowo.[1]

Table 6.1 indicates the number of divorces, not just divorcees, during each of three periods: reign I, the beginning of reign III, and after the initial period in which marriage was reestablished during reign III. The total figures are 23 and 26 respectively for men and women. This is higher than the number of divorcees shown previously; the discrepancy can be explained by the fact that two of the men have been divorced twice, one of the women three times, and four other women twice. Thus the actual number of divorcees for men and women remains 21 and 20, respectively.

TABLE 6.1. NUMBER OF DIVORCES DURING THE THREE PERIODS

	men	women
reign I	1	2
beginning of reign III	20	20
after initial divorce at the beginning of reign III	2	4
TOTAL	23	26

One factor must be stressed. No person was divorced more than once during the interval starting with the reign of the second *oba* and finishing with the resumption of a formal marital bond when the third *oba* came to the throne. Therefore the total number of divorces for that period is equal to the total number of divorcees for the period. In other words 20 of the 31 men and 20 of the 27 women became divorced shortly after the third *oba* took the throne.

This proportion is high. But it can be demonstrated that the true divorce rate at that time was even more extensive than indicated so far. Of the 10 men who were not divorced, only three actually were married before the third *oba* became king. The other seven were young. Their average age in 1970 was 30. All of them married when the third *oba* introduced the formal bond in 1966, which means they were only 25 years old at the time of marriage. Thus only 24 men (21 + 3) were actually married before marriage was banned by the second *oba*. The true divorce rate for the sample when the third *oba* introduced marriage again, then, is 20 out of 24, or 83% of the men.

---

[1]The figures for all the tables in this chapter except 6.3, 6.9, and 6.10 are derived from a small questionnaire used to investigate residence and marriage patterns. Simple random samples of 10% of the 137 houses in the male sector and 13% of the 76 houses in the female sector that were completed for the general questionnaire were selected. These amounted to 14 and 10 houses respectively.

The family and marriage were perhaps the most sensitive subjects in Olowo, and when questions were asked about them people often became close-lipped if not hostile. For this reason I used the technique described in the preface: after the samples were selected, a questionnaire excluding attitudinal variables was erected, and the services of a trusted informant obtained.

With regard to the women, seven have not been divorced. Only two of these were married before the third *oba* took over. The remaining five became married in 1966 for the first time. Their average age in 1970 was 22.6, which means they were only 17 when they married. Of the two women not divorced, but married before the present *oba* came to the throne, both were older and had been married for several years. One of them had been married twice. But in her case it was because her first husband died. For the 27 women, then, only 22 (27–5) were married before 1966. The true divorce rate for the sample of women in 1966, thus, is 20 out of 22, or 91%.[2]

The reestablishment of a formal marital bond, accompanied by the high divorce rate, is only one of two significant changes that took place with respect to marriage after the third *oba* came to the throne. The other change concerns polygyny. As indicated in Chapter 1, with the exception of the *oba* almost everybody during the reign of the first leader had no more than one wife. After 1966 polygyny was introduced. The number of wives possessed by a sample of men before and after 1966 is shown in Table 6.2. The difference is only a modest one.

TABLE 6.2. NUMBER OF WIVES BEFORE AND AFTER 1966

	married men	wives
before 1966	24	25
after 1966[a]	24	29

[a]Seven men in the sample who were not married prior to 1966 are excluded.

It was learned that the majority of changes in the community have been conditioned by the status factor. It was speculated that the increase in the number of wives might also be affected by it. Thus the three categories of different status that were employed in the Introduction were used again. As indicated in Table 6.3, the number of wives possessed by the men in all three categories was almost identical before 1966. But after 1966 there was a significant increase among the highest status group: an increase from an average of 1.2 to 4.6 wives. Therefore the precise rate of increase in polygyny cannot be detected unless the status variable is introduced.

A problem arises in the data because not only has there been an increase in the number of wives among high-status men, but there was also an increase (albeit modest) in the other two status categories as well.

If the elite now have more wives, does this not mean the remainder of the men will have less? The answer is no, and this is because of a change in policy toward outsiders. After the initial settlement in 1947, there was great hostility between the new community and the villages that surrounded it. As a result there were

---

[2]Lloyd (1966 and 1968) suggests that the divorce rate among the Yoruba is high. He traces it to two main factors: the economic independence of the wife from her husband and the fact that she is only slightly alienated from her own descent group.

TABLE 6.3. NUMBER OF WIVES BEFORE AND AFTER 1966 ACCORDING TO STATUS

	high status		upper-middle status		low status	
	(10 actors)		(12 actors)		(20 actors)	
	n	%	n	%	n	%
before 1966	12	1.2	12	1.0	20	1.0
after 1966	46	4.6	19	1.6	22	1.1

few recruits from 1947 onwards. Toward the end of the reign of the first *oba* the social distance decreased, and he was apparently in favor of inviting more people to join, although few responded. During the reign of the second *oba* the village was in turmoil. Rather than an increase in new members, there was a loss of established members. When the third *oba* assumed office, he made it clear that new recruits would be welcomed. This supposedly included both men and women, but in actuality only the latter were sought. Olowo has been quite successful with its new policy. Numerous women have joined recently, presumably attracted to this wealthy, modern village in the midst of hardship.

Child-Rearing

It has been explained that after the age of five or six most children went to live with an adult of the same sex other than their own parent, having been claimed at the kindergarten. There was considerable unhappiness with this system, for children were employed as servants and sometimes badly treated.

The current *oba* was aware of the dissatisfaction among his flock. When he took office he introduced two modifications. First, while children still must attend the kindergarten, the two men in charge no longer have the authority to distribute them among adults. Instead, the permission of the child's mother and father must be obtained. Secondly, the *oba* announced that a child could now live with his or her own father or mother. The *oba* is said to have made these changes not only because of the unhappiness of parents, but also because he had concluded that the old system had not worked. Its purpose was to produce a well-trained child, but misbehavior continued to be rampant. He thought a child's own parents would be able to do a better job. My own interpretation is that the children's misbehavior was not the main cause of the change. Instead the new policy was a response to the growing feeling of family solidarity in the village.

Residence Patterns

Given the significant changes in the marriage system since 1966, as well as the *oba*'s desire to modify the child-rearing practices, I assumed that changes in residence patterns also would follow. Two hypotheses were formulated:

1. Since 1966 a higher proportion of spouses have begun to live together.
2. Since 1966 a higher proportion of children have begun to live with their parents of the same sex.

An analysis was made of the residence patterns of the people drawn in the samples used to investigate divorce and polygyny. The initial hypothesis can be considered and discarded immediately: not one case of co-residence of spouses was uncovered. Thus I go on now to consider the second hypothesis.

Table 6.4 indicates the number of houses in the samples drawn from the male and female sectors that contain at least two people related by kin. Almost two-thirds of the houses in the male sector contain no relatives; but in the female sector nine of the 10 houses have at least two people related.

TABLE 6.4. NUMBER OF HOUSES CONTAINING AT LEAST
TWO PEOPLE RELATED BY KINSHIP

	male		female	
	n	%	n	%
relatives	5	36	9	90
number of relatives	9	64	1	10
TOTAL	14	100	10	100

a_{x^2} (1 df) = 10.42, thus significant at .01 level.

Table 6.5 presents the same data in another form. It shows that 32% and 67% of the males and females respectively live in a house with at least one other relative. It is important to present the data in this manner as well, for the fact that 90% of the houses in the female sector contain at least one kin tie does not mean 90% of those in each house are related to each other.

TABLE 6.5. NUMBER OF PEOPLE RELATED TO AT LEAST
ONE OTHER PERSON IN HOUSE

	male		female	
	n	%	n	%
related	17	32.7	27	67.5
not related	36	67.8	13	32.5
TOTAL	53	100.5	40	100.0

a_{x^2} (1 df) = 20.57, thus significant at .01 level.

Table 6.6 shows the exact relationship among those who live in the five houses containing relatives in the male sector. Only 17 of the 24 men involved are related to at least one other person. The most frequent tie is to the landlords; four are their sons, three are their sisters' sons, and one is the son of a landlord's brother. Of the five others who are related to someone other than the landlord two are brothers, and the remaining three consist of a man and his two sons who live in a house where the adult is not the landlord.

TABLE 6.6. RELATIONSHIPS OF THE 24 PERSONS IN FIVE HOUSES IN
THE MALE SECTOR CONTAINING RELATIVES

	related	not related
tenants related to landlords	8	
landlords related to tenants	4	
tenants related to other tenants	5	
landlords not related to any tenants		1
tenants not related to anyone else		6
TOTALS	17	7

Table 6.7 summarizes the relationships among those who live in the nine houses containing relatives in the female sector. Only 27 of the 37 involved are related. Again the most frequent tie is to the household head. Of the 12 people related to the landladies, seven are their daughters, three their granddaughters, one a sister, and the last the sister's daughter. Most of those who are related to somebody other than the landlady are mother and daughter, or son under the age of five or six.

TABLE 6.7. RELATIONSHIPS OF THE 37 PERSONS IN NINE HOUSES IN
THE FEMALE SECTOR CONTAINING RELATIVES

	related	not related
tenants related to landladies	12	
landladies related to tenants	5	
tenants related to other tenants	10	
landladies not related to any tenants		4
tenants not related to anyone else		6
TOTALS	27	10

The data were gathered in 1970, and represent residence patterns that existed at that time. But to what extent were these patterns established after the third *oba* came to the throne in 1966? Table 6.8 indicates the length of residence of the 53 males and 40 females in the houses represented in the samples. As it is shown, 78% and 80% of the male and female populace have lived in the same house for at least five years, thus predating the reign of the present *oba*. Since 40% and 48% respectively of the men and women have not changed residence for over 10 years, it can be concluded that there was considerable stability in terms of long-range residence in the community.

Yet 22% of the males and 20% of the females have lived in their present house less than 6 years. This high proportion suggests the possibility that residence patterns have changed significantly. However, an examination of the cases included among those of less than 5 years of residence reveals that the figures are deceptive.

Of the 12 males, only five are over 10 years old. Four of these five are non-members, who live with an older relative employed by the community. Only one is a member who actually has changed houses within the male sector. He moved because his former home was overcrowded. Seven of the boys are under

TABLE 6.8. LENGTH OF RESIDENCE

	male		female	
	n	%	n	%
less than 6 years	12	22.6	8	20.0
6–10 years	20	37.7	13	32.5
11–23 years	21	39.7	19	47.5
TOTAL	53	100.0	40	100.0

10 years old. It has been explained that boys move over to the male sector after the age of five or six. This simple fact, thus, accounts for their brief residence, and cannot be used as an index of a change in policy with regard to residence.

Of the eight females who have lived in their houses less than 6 years, only two are over 6 years old, and one of them is 8 years old. She moved from her mother's house to one that contained no relatives. The other is 18 years old. She is a newcomer to the village, which explains her brief residence. Since the remaining six girls are less than 6 years old, this simple fact accounts for their short residence. Finally, while the number of cases that I gathered for both before and after 1966 is not sufficient to warrant a detailed report, I found no evidence of a greater tendency since 1966 for boys to move across to their father's house at the age of six, or for girls at this age to remain in their mother's house. Moreover, there was no evidence that either boys or girls who had already moved into the house of a nonrelative before 1966 have since then begun to move back to their mother's house; or in the case of boys, to their father's house. What this means is that the estimate that over 20% of Olowo people have changed residence since 1966 is indeed deceptive.

The research findings, therefore, are in conflict with the two hypotheses. First, there has not been a tendency for husband and wife to co-reside. Second, there has not been a tendency for children to begin to live with the parent of the same sex. Given this information, it can be assumed that the estimates of the proportion of people who live in a house containing at least one other kinsman (32.1% and 67.9% respectively for male and female) hold both for 1970 and the past.

The nature of residence patterns in Olowo was discovered primarily from the samples drawn from the male and female sectors. In addition, a minor project was undertaken to see whether lines are organized according to kin. From impressions gathered during the previous months this seemed unlikely. For this reason only one line in each sector was selected. In the male line there were eight houses, containing 34 residents; in the female line there were eight houses, with 31 residents.

As indicated in Table 6.9, only six kinship ties exist in the male line between people in different houses. This is out of a total possible number of 503 ties, given every person on the line related to everyone else. The figure for the female line is even lower. Only one kinship tie between people in different houses in the line exists. It is concluded, then, that lines in the community are not organized upon a kinship basis. There is a simple explanation why more men than women are related to others in houses in the same line. As shown previously, there is a greater tendency for women to live with relatives in the same house. The men must live somewhere: inevitably a greater proportion of them will live in the same line as their relatives.

TABLE 6.9. RESIDENCE BY LINE: NUMBER OF
KINSHIP RELATIONS AMONG PEOPLE NOT LIVING IN
THE SAME HOUSE

	total no. of possible relations	actual no. of relations
male	503	6
female	389	1

[a]Figures are arrived at by counting all the possible relationships of each of the 34 males and 31 females to all others in the line not living in the same house.

A secondary aspect of the line residence project was to see how many relatives were living in each house, rather than in different houses. This was intended as a check on the previous residence project. Six of the eight houses in the male sector and seven of the eight in the female sector contain at least two people who are related to each other. The proportion fits with that derived from the earlier project for the women, but is higher than that for the men. In the more extensive project a simple random sample was drawn, and can be accepted as more valid. Further, when the figures are broken down to determine the exact number of people related in each of the houses in the two lines, the trends arrived at in the previous project are more closely approximated. In the six houses with relatives in the male line, only two contain more than two relatives. In the seven houses in the female line with relatives, five contain more than two people who are related. The greater tendency for women to live with their own relatives thus is reinforced.

Residence and Stratification

Given the major changes in marriage in Olowo since 1966, as well as the proposals by the *oba* to modify the system of child-rearing, it was anticipated that there would be accompanying changes in residence patterns. The data did not support the assumption. Husband and wife have not started to live together, nor have children begun to live with their parents on an increased scale.

It will be recalled that it was only when the status variable was introduced that the range of increase in polygyny since 1966 could be detected. This might mean that residence patterns also may have been modified according to status, thus rendering the previous projects insensitive to the change. In order to develop this assumption, the three categories of different status that were used on previous occasions were relied on once more: high, upper-middle, and low status. Two hypotheses were formulated:

1. The higher the status of a man, the greater the tendency for his wife (or wives) to live with him.
2. The higher the status of a man, the greater the tendency for his children to live with him.

The results are presented in Table 6.10. With respect to the initial hypothesis, six of the 10 men in the highest status group have some of their wives living with them, while none of those in the lowest status category enjoy this privilege: and it must be interpreted as a privilege insomuch as it is more frequent among those of high status. Unfortunately I do not have comparative data for the period prior to the present reign. However, I am confident that the tendency for husband and wife to live together is a recent phenomenon. All informants have stressed that this is so.

The initial hypothesis therefore is confirmed, but with one qualification. Only a single person of upper-middle status lives with his wife (he has only one). This is lower than was anticipated for this category. Therefore the hypothesis that co-residence of spouses varies directly with status holds primarily for the two extreme status categories.

TABLE 6.10. RESIDENCE AND STRATIFICATION SINCE 1966

	Does wife live in same house as husband?			*Does child live in same house as father?*		
	yes		no	yes		no
	all wives	some wives		all children	some children	
high status (10 actors)	0	6	4	3	6	1
upper-middle status (12 actors)	1	0	11	0	3	8
low status (20 actors)	0	0	20	1	3	16
TOTAL	1	6	35	4	12	25

As regards the second hypothesis, nine of the 10 people of high status, three of the 12 of upper-middle status, and four of the 20 of low status have at least one of their children living with them. To put this in percentage terms, 90%, 25% and 20% of the three status groups enjoy this privilege. Once more we are confronted with the lack of comparable data for the same people in the past. All that I can do is stress that both member and nonmember informants have impressed upon me that the children of important people have started to live with their own mothers or fathers on a large scale since the third *oba* came to the throne.

The second hypothesis therefore is accepted, but it too must be qualified. As in the case of co-residence of spouses, there is very little difference between the proportions for the upper-middle and low-status groups: 25% and 20% respectively have at least one child living with them. This hypothesis too, then, holds only for the extremes of highest and lowest status.

A further qualification must be made. The status categories were drawn from the male sector. This imposes considerable limitations. For example, a man's children may live with his wife rather than with him. This is especially so if they are girls, or boys under the age of six. The only positive note is that the same limitations extend to all three status groups. Unless the tendency for children of high-status people to live with their father is not replicated among the women, the results should be reliable. I have no reason to assume that the trend among the women is any different.

Conclusion

The creation of a formal marital bond and the tendency of relatives of high status to live together suggest that the Olowo family has begun to emerge as a legitimate institution. We are now in a position to consider two of the assumptions that were introduced in Chapter 2. There it was argued that the importance of the family at the beginning was even *less* than suggested by its structural properties, and since 1966 is even *more* than these suggest. The relevant structural properties are the proportion of spouses and offspring co-residing and the presence or absence of a formal marital bond.

The first part of the assumption has already been confirmed. As previously explained, while a formal marital bond existed for most of the first *oba*'s reign, a certain proportion of relatives lived together, and members knew the identity of their relatives, all activities organized according to family ties were prohibited.

As regards the second part of the assumption, the family has become stronger since 1966 from a structural point of view. Once more marriage has become legitimate; and also husband and wife, and in some cases their children, have begun to live together. How can it be argued, then, that in 1970 the family was *more* important than suggested structurally?

The explanation concerns the other assumption left undeveloped in Chapter 2. This is the argument that there has been a change from kinship identification to kinship consciousness. The structural changes in the family have been limited to people of high status. Yet kinship consciousness is endemic throughout the social structure, for regardless of status Olowo people are beginning to order their universe according to their family ties. Indeed, in the next chapter it will be shown that the family is emerging as an economic unit. Relatives are gathering together to purchase boats and motors for fishing, and keeping the profits for the family. The implication is that the structural changes do not reflect the significance of family ties in Olowo today, for they are limited to high-status people.

Given the transition from kinship identity to consciousness, two predictions can be made. The first is that in the future co-residence of spouses and children will extend to the entire populace, rather than remain limited to the elite. In other words the discrepancy between a value variable (the consciousness of family) and a structural variable (the proportion of relatives living together) will be resolved.

The second prediction concerns the family substitutes. It is predicted that as the family emerges in strength, these structures will cease to fulfil a family function. But they will not cease to exist. This is because they did not emerge in order to act as family substitutes. Instead their functions expanded in order to fill the vacuum created by the suppression of the family.

Finally, my purpose has been to document the numerous changes that have occurred in marriage and the family in recent years. Just as significant, perhaps, are those features that have *not* changed: for example marriage ritual. In the past there was no ritual; instead the *oba* merely announced the union of two people in the church. This aspect of marriage has not changed. However, one incident suggests that it may in the future. In 1970 the *oba* decided to celebrate his most recent marriage about two months after it had occurred. The ritual to be established would set the standard for all subsequent marriages in the village. The palace courtyard was prepared for the event, and outsiders such as the leader of Talika were invited. There was much merriment, but there was no marriage ritual as such. Nor did marriages among ordinary members after this event include any celebration.

The *oba* said that he decided to celebrate his marriage because outsiders insist that without a proper ritual a person is not married. The outsiders also say that because there are no ceremonies there is no fun in Olowo. The *oba* told his subjects that there is nothing wrong with celebrating marriage, and that it should be done in order to prove to outsiders that they do enjoy life.

Perhaps a more valid explanation concerns the woman involved in the ceremony. She is a newcomer to the village. My impression was that her father, a clergyman, was quite upset that his daughter did not have a conventional Christian marriage. The inference is that the ceremony at the palace was intended to placate the woman's father by showing that marriage was a formal and ritual event. The fact that the celebration took place two months after the marriage itself lends support to this argument.

It would be wrong, then, to assume that this one celebration marks a change in marriage procedure. Marriage still does not involve any ritual, any formal legal procedure (either customary or civil law), or any biblical content. The consequences of this for the manner in which members regard marriage is reflected in the words of one young married man. Pondering over their system, he once queried aloud: "Am I married?"

7. Discussion: Economic and Family Changes

The structures of the economy and the family have been transformed in the last few years. These changes can be looked at from two perspectives. One is the point of view of the Olowo people themselves, who say that both changes were intended to reduce strain in the village. We shall see to what extent this aim was achieved. The other perspective is that of the observer. I shall argue first that the changes in the family were a consequence of the introduction of private enterprise. I shall then offer a more general explanation within which both the economic and family changes can be subsumed. Finally, I shall return once more to a comparison of Olowo with the kibbutz.

As regards the people's interpretation, the third *oba* once referred to the state of affairs that existed in Olowo before he came to office. According to him, his subjects had grown lazy. Many of the most industrious of the founders of the community had become old men, no longer providing inspiration. Furthermore, the community had become corrupt. Members stole from each other and sold the goods in neighboring villages. In order to rectify the laziness and corruption a change of some kind was required.

The *oba*'s subjects agreed that corruption was widespread. They also stated that people did not show up for work in the departments, let alone go to work on the seashore before their regular job began. However, they did not explain this in terms of laziness. Instead they said they were tired of working so hard for little direct personal reward. Some of them added that they were hostile toward the elite who walked around the village wearing magnificent robes.

The introduction of private money was intended to put an end to the laziness, corruption, and jealousy. According to informants the attitude toward work has changed dramatically. It is a fact, for example, that the seashore now is crowded in the early morning by both men and women. Even many of the elders have begun to work again. Their willingness does not mean they have accepted the new economic system. Instead it is a question of necessity since the community no longer provides them with all they need.

My general impression, then, coincides with the remarks of my informants. The village appears to have been revitalized. Indeed, it is probably accurate to describe it as having entered a second take-off stage. While problems such as "laziness" have been resolved, this does not mean there no longer is conflict in the village in relation to economic affairs. Indeed, the structural change in the economy has generated a new type of tension. There is now a tendency for people to refuse to work unless they are more highly rewarded. In other words they want to increase the range of private enterprise in the village.

Numerous cases were observed that support this statement. One of them concerns the shoe department. During the Nigerian civil war it was not possible to obtain the raw material needed for the factory. For this reason it ceased to be an important source of income. After the war ended in January 1970, the manager of the factory arranged to sell as many shoes as they could make to a large wholesale company on the mainland.

When he tried to begin production, however, he ran into obstacles. The workers decided that their bonus for 1969 had been too small and refused to cooperate. The manager was desperate, for the wholesale company had requested 1000 shoes by the end of the month. He offered to pay the workers 1 pound per day. They agreed and for a brief period the shoe factory was a place of frenzied activity. But it ended suddenly when the manager changed his mind and decided not to pay them. The workers again refused to cooperate.

This resulted in two events. First, the manager reported the matter to the *oba* and requested permission to hire outsiders. Permission was granted and eight young men from surrounding villages were recruited. The second event was the punishment of the regular workers. A meeting was arranged with the *oba* as chairman. Four of the shoemakers were accused of laziness and disobedience, and were flogged publicly.

In explaining the legitimation of marriage and the family, members of Olowo referred to the disorder that existed during the reign of the second *oba*. The major cause, they argued, was the absence of marriage. Competition for sexual partners apparently was intense, and exhausted a considerable part of each day. One result was that the economy broke down, for people no longer reported promptly to their departments in the morning. The present *oba* established marriage once more in order to reduce the disorder in the village.

What has been the result? It has already been reported that the economy now thrives. It is difficult to estimate the precise contribution of the legitimation of marriage and the family, given the accompanying introduction of private enterprise. But competition for sexual partners remains a major source of conflict. This conflict is both external and internal. By external I mean relations between Olowo and the outside world. By internal I mean conflict that is generated primarily among members of Olowo themselves.

The external conflict concerns the new policy of recruiting women. As indicated earlier, this policy was necessary in order that polygyny could be introduced without forcing low-status people to remain bachelors. The policy has been very successful. Indeed, the *oba* remarked one day in church that they were getting back all the women who previously escaped—or at least their equivalent.

Olowo recognizes certain obligations toward the former husband of a woman who joins the community. He is paid 30 pounds in compensation, although this is not automatic. The community sometimes withholds the brideprice until there has been an opportunity to see if the girl will fit into the village. In spite of the willingness to compensate the husband for the loss of his wife, the energetic recruitment policy has generated much conflict between Olowo and the surrounding villages. Women who have quarreled with their husbands often flee to Olowo. The outsiders accuse Olowo of deceiving these women with gifts and sweet words, and at times try to get their women back.

In a recent case, for example, a girl who had joined Olowo only a few months before was seized from her canoe by two men about three miles from the community. One was her former husband. Some Olowo boys saw what happened, and quickly paddled home. After the news spread there was pandemonium. Led by the deputy *oba*, a group of angry men went after the two men in one of the village's speedboats. The house where the girl was taken was discovered. She was released, and her captors were forcibly taken to Olowo. For a while they were tied up in the community guard house. Finally, they were taken to see the *oba*, who condemned their behavior but allowed them to leave the village unharmed.

Internal strain is more severe. A minor source concerns the recruitment of outsiders. Longstanding female members tend to be hostile to the recruits— especially when the latter become their junior wives. This reaction has been so widespread that the *oba* has found it necessary to warn the women to treat the newcomers as friends.

A further minor source of strain from the recruitment policy exists. Olowo men are encouraged to recruit all the women they can. However, the men who persuade the women to join are not always allowed to keep them as their wives. I know of four cases in which women joined with the purpose of marrying a specific man, but were forced to marry someone else. In one case of this in 1969, the new recruit finally agreed to marry the man chosen for her after the *oba* promised her many gifts.

The major source of internal conflict at present, however, concerns marriage fidelity. The village places great emphasis upon this ideal, yet adultery is widespread. In recognition of this, the *oba* recently introduced a further innovation, albeit a minor one. Before 1966, and excluding of course those periods when marriage was banned entirely, one's spouse was chosen by the *oba*. The husband, but not the wife, is said to have been able to reject the *oba*'s choice if he did not approve. Faced with the fact that male-female relations remain the major source of internal conflict, the *oba* decided to give the choice of partner to the women. In some cases, however, a woman may be ordered to choose her husband from a specific group of men, or to marry a man whom the *oba* wishes to reward.

As in the case of the economic innovation, the changes in marriage and the family have generated a new type of tension in Olowo. Evidence of this concerning marriage has already been given: the quarrels with hostile husbands whose wives have joined the village. Evidence concerning the family also exists. For example, in 1970 one young man accused members of a particular family of trying to make their family the strongest and wealthiest in the village. Two members of the family are among the best educated people in the village. They vigorously denied the accusation. But as the accuser told me, everyone is now trying to improve the position of his family.

With this in mind, a prediction can be added to those made at the end of Chapter 6. Not only will residence patterns change throughout the stratification system, and family substitutes cease to function in this way, but the family will become a major source of internal conflict. If this materializes, it will hasten the end of the communal social organization. For as was stated earlier, the family and the communal system are rival phenomena.

I have indicated how Olowo people themselves explain the recent economic and family changes, and have considered the degree to which the changes have resolved the strain that apparently preceded them. The analysis will shift now from the actor's to the observer's interpretation.

I shall begin by trying to show that the changes in the family were partly a consequence of the changes in the economy. The evidence is twofold. First, as indicated at the end of Chapter 5, the family is emerging as an economic unit. It will be recalled that three distinct organizational units of work emerged in Olowo, and that one of them became entirely organized along private enterprise lines after the third *oba* assumed office. This is the individual work carried out when people are not involved with the departments or with communal labor. This private work is increasingly becoming family-dominated. For example, relatives have begun to pool their resources to purchase sea-going canoes for fishing.

The present *oba* has strongly supported this development. He argues that his subjects no longer should expect handouts from the community, and often reminds them that if they were living outside Olowo they would be hard pressed to support themselves. He specifically encourages relatives to be responsible for the welfare of each other.

The tendency for the family to become an economic unit is only one indication that the changes in the family were a function of the changes in the economy. A second one concerns stratification. In Chapter 4 it was shown that a direct consequence of the introduction of private enterprise was an increase in material rewards along status lines. In Chapter 5 it was shown that also along status lines there has been an increase in the number of wives per man, and in the number of marriage partners and their children living together. My argument is that the latter changes are comparable to those concerning material rewards and complement them. Indeed, wives and children in this context may be considered to be as material as the rewards of bicycles, record players, and radios.

There is a simple explanation why this second type of reward exists. As it has been indicated, the range of private enterprise in the community is limited. The amount of money one can accumulate from all sources is small. Yet the *oba* has declared that those who contribute the most must be rewarded correspondingly. One way to do so is to give them a bicycle or a radio. Another is to give them more than one wife, or to allow them to live with their wives and children. Thus, this type of reward not only reflects the widening of the stratification system in

Olowo, but also suggests a further means by which the *oba* continues to manipulate the system as he wishes.

The emergence of the family as a legitimate institution, then, would seem to be partly a consequence of the changes in the economy. I now want to raise the level of abstraction in order to explain both the economic and family changes within a single framework. These changes can be described as part of a process of normalization, the term used in reference to both Olowo and the kibbutz at the end of Chapter 4.[1]

My basic assumption is that no society, institution, or value system is more normal than another in any ultimate sense. Instead the normal assumes a specific meaning only in social context. Moreover, normalization is a power phenomenon. It is a process by which a dominant social entity (a region, a village, or even a value orientation) impinges upon and reshapes a weaker social entity.

The normalization model is intended specifically for the analysis of the dynamics involved between an aberrant social system and its larger setting. In as much as Olowo is an anomaly in Ilaje, the village must eventually embrace the structural and value patterns of its setting. The partial replacement of communalism by private enterprise and the increase in polygyny were not random events. Both of these are features of Olowo's setting. Nor were they a result of an evolutionary process, for if this was the case we would have expected monogamy to emerge, as it has generally throughout industrial societies.

Two problems arise. First, is it not possible that the unit will dominate its setting, with the result that the direction of change will be reversed? Certainly Olowo has had a profound impact on Ilaje as a whole. In spite of the hostility of the surrounding villages, they aspire to the rapid development displayed by Olowo. Nevertheless, as the example of other utopias such as the kibbutz suggests (Talmon-Garber 1962), the fire that feeds the energy of the Olowo people will eventually die, and with it resistance to the outside world.

Second, what precisely is meant by setting? In outlining the procedure for structural-functional requisite analysis, Levy (1952) gives the impression that setting is not an ambiguous term. Yet it has at least two dimensions: physical and sociological. In the case of Olowo, the physical setting may be said to be Ilaje, Yoruba territory, Nigeria as a whole, or all of West Africa. The cut-off point seems to be completely arbitrary.

The sociological dimension concerns Olowo's reference groups. In as much as normalization involves attitudes, it is relevant to know the groups that are references for the village. Ilaje is a negative reference group; the modernizing Nigerian mainland is a positive reference group. But Olowo people often refer to Europe

---

[1]Before I began research in Olowo in 1969, I anticipated that the community would be undergoing tremendous change at that time. One of the three models taken to the field focused upon this problem. While similar in some respects to the "normalization" model, it is not presented here because the appropriate data to examine it have been excluded from this book.

and America as well. Indeed, they sometimes call Olowo "the little London" of Nigeria. Again it seems arbitrary what one defines as the setting.

These are not the only problems with the normalization model. While it explains the *direction* of change, it does not explain *when* normalization will take place. In order to do so, we must know two further variables. The first is a general requisite for this type of analysis. It concerns the duration of the utopia's existence. The time factor is important because change is likely to occur a generation or so after it was founded. This is long enough for the message of the utopia to lose its urgency. Moreover, the new generation will have learned about the birth pains only second-hand.

The second variable is a requisite specifically for the case of Olowo. It concerns royal succession. Its significance for the many major changes in economic and family organization has been implied throughout the preceeding chapters. The tendency for these changes to follow the succession of the second and third *obas* is not fortuitous. This is because strains tend to accumulate in a social system until a change of leadership occurs. This does not have to be a case of royal succession. As Gouldner (1954) shows, it can involve a change of managers in a factory. It must be stressed that succession does not *cause* change. Instead it acts as a trigger mechanism. Tensions that have accumulated are released during periods of succession.

In summary, the structural changes in both the economy and the family took place because Olowo is an anomaly in Ilaje. The changes were in the direction of the social structure of the setting because the latter defines what is normal. The changes occurred at this particular time because the community has existed for about a generation, and because this time span coincided with royal succession.[2]

Throughout this study my argument has been that the changes in the family were dependent upon the changes in the economy. First it was shown that the suppression of the family followed the replacement of capitalism by communalism in 1948. Then it was shown that the emergence of the family as a legitimate institution followed the partial replacement of communalism by capitalism after

---

[2]Several other concepts could have been used in place of normalization: rationalization, secularization, routinization, secondary institutionalization, and adaptation. By "rationalization" Weber (1965) seems to have meant numerous ideas, such as a tendency toward internal logical consistency of value systems, the empirical testing of ideas, and systematic procedure in the solution of problems (bureaucracy). Because it cannot be assumed that bureaucratic procedures, rationality, and empiricism are features of Olowo's setting, normalization is a more appropriate concept. The same can be said about "secularization," for the direction of change could be toward greater religiosity, if this was a dominant feature of the environment.

"Routinization" and "normalization" are both used by Talmon (1965) to describe changes in the kibbutz comparable to those in Olowo. My only reluctance about routinization is that it connotes to me the consolidation of power and values, rather than the radical changes such as the adoption of private enterprise in Olowo. Weintraub, *et al.* (1969) use "secondary institutionalization" in reference to the kibbutz, and Parsons (1951, chap. XI) employs "adaptation" to describe postrevolutionary activity. Both of these would seem to be as satisfactory as "normalization."

1966. It is true that the tendency of the family to act as an economic unit is a recent phenomenon—probably since 1969. Yet I am not certain that the creation of a formal marital bond and the emergence of polygyny came after the structural modification of the economy. All that is clear is that both the economic and family changes occurred after the third *oba* assumed office. For this reason it is more appropriate to portray the changes in each institution as mutually interdependent. The normalization model again would appear to be relevant, for it does not assign causal primacy to either structure.

One other possible explanation of the changes in economic and family organization concerns the personal attributes of the present *oba*. Previously it was suggested that quite apart from the high degree of authority in his role, the personality of the first *oba* contributed to the establishment of communalism and the suppression of the family. It is not argued that the recent economic and family changes were the brainchild of the present *oba*. These changes were generated from existing social conditions. However, the present *oba* probably was instrumental in the successful adaptation of the community to these major changes. While he does not command the same awe from his subjects as did the first *oba*, he has an outstanding flair for organization. It is likely that his intelligent and sensitive leadership helped to guide the innovations into the village in a manner that minimized strain.

Conclusion

In conclusion, Olowo can again be compared with the kibbutz. It was shown earlier that the communal economic system, the suppression of the family, and the emergence of family substitutes are common to both communities. It will now be shown that the recent changes in the Olowo economy and family also have their counterpart in the kibbutzim.

As in Olowo, private enterprise has infiltrated the kibbutz: for example, some people work for wages outside the community, which enables them to purchase objects such as radios (Spiro 1963, p. 206). Kibbutz members have also begun to demand their own private property. Spiro (1963, p. 209) sums up the changes in the community he studied as follows: "There seems to be little doubt that Kiryat Yedidim is in the midst of a general trend from a completely community-centered society to one in which there is a much greater degree of privacy." This trend toward privacy, as reflected in both economic and family relations, is found in Olowo as well.

With the exception of polygyny as the marital form, the changes in marriage and the family also have paralleled those in Olowo. In the past an effort was made to avoid using the terms husband and wife. Now they are commonplace, and the family is emerging as an important social unit. Indeed, Talmon (1965, pp. 280–281) states that the most significant change in the kibbutz family is the re-emergence of wider kinship ties, both within the community itself and with relatives living outside the kibbutz. It is noteworthy that a similar trend is found in two other cases in which the family supposedly does not exist: the Nayars and the Soviet Union. Mencher (1965, pp. 177–178) has reported that among the former a recognizable marriage and family system has emerged in the last few decades. And Geiger (1968, p. 329) has shown that Russian leaders no longer talk about the withering away of the family.

I return once more to Murdock's work. Does the emergence of strong family ties in all these cases mean that it is impossible to do away with the family? This is the conclusion that Firth (1964, p. 71) arrived at in reference to the kibbutz and the U.S.S.R. Geiger's observations (1968, p. 323) with regard to the Soviet family are highly relevant:

. . . on the age-old issue of whether a society can do without the family, the history of the Soviet family does not appear to provide an answer. There was no real Soviet effort to replace the family, because other tasks and demands were so pressing that basic functions, child-rearing, food production, and the like, could not be sponsored by public agencies on a sufficiently large scale. Consequently we would be ill-advised to ring down the curtain in the fashion proposed by some observers, who hold that the Soviet rulers "tried to abolish the family but failed, which proves that the family is indispensable." Nothing of the sort, and the question is still a legitimate one.

This conclusion clashes with Firth's observation, but I am inclined to accept it—not only for the Soviet case, but for the kibbutz and Olowo as well. In none of these cases was the family abolished completely. Hence its gradual legitimation does not mean that the family can never be replaced.

Even the emergence of the family among the Nayars may not prove that it is impossible to do without the family. While stressing that the Nayars case is more extreme than the kibbutz in terms of the degree to which the family and marriage in the past were absent, Mogey (1962, p. 412) points out that ". . . the recognition of the husband by a ritual marriage ceremony and a death ceremony establishes the legitimacy of his position and therefore the existence of parental if not marital status within the society." In this case, too, then, an aspect of family phenomenon may always have existed.

Apart from the economic and family spheres, other changes are common to Olowo and the kibbutz. In the latter older women have begun to dye their hair. In the former women have begun to wear earrings. Such behavior in each community would have been scandalous in the past. Both are signs of normalization. A more significant change that they share concerns the political realm. Although Spiro modifies his argument in the preface to the second edition of his work, in the original he says that the kibbutz has changed from a "withdrawing" to a "militant" sect, in which it aspires to modify the outside world in its own image. A similar change occurred in Olowo. For the initial 20 years it withdrew from the villages that surrounded it. Then it suddenly tried to gain political control over these villages, which is what the branch movement resulting in the union with Talika signifies.

A general trend in both communities, then, emerges along the dimensions of the economic, the kinship, and the political. Other social movements such as the cargo cults would also seem to fit at least the political dimension. As many authors have noted (for example, Worsley, 1970), there is a tendency for these cults eventually to be transformed into incipient political organizations. The implication is that Olowo, the kibbutz, and perhaps other cases, can be subsumed within a single sociological type which will enable us to predict their social structural development.[3] In other words, a theory can be developed around a specific social field. As Gluckman (1963, p. 82) would argue, this is the end toward which anthropology should strive. That normalization, or a comparable term, will constitute an important concept for the theory is not surprising. For as Spiro (1963, p. 215) remarks, ". . . no one can live in a permanent revolution."

---

[3]For attempts to formulate a theory of social movements of this nature, see Wallace (1956) and Linton (1943).

Part Three

THE FAMILY AND INDUSTRIALIZATION

BOWLING GREEN STATE UNIVERSITY LIBRARY

8. The Family in Talika

Talika was founded in 1951 by disillusioned members of Olowo. For almost 20 years there was no formal contact between them. Then in 1969 Talika accepted Olowo's invitation to become a branch community.[1] In this chapter the family in Talika will be described in order to provide comparative material for Olowo, and to set the stage for considering the significance of both villages for a body of theory that has so far been ignored. This is the literature that deals with the relationship between family type and economic development.

I shall begin by describing the marriage system and residence patterns. I shall then consider the consequences of the union with Olowo for the family. As it will be shown, the Talika family has been stable since the village was founded. The only major change in recent years is that the *oba* has attempted to remove the incest taboo. But this factor is not connected to the union with Olowo, and has even less significance for the relationship of the family to industrialization.

The main reason why the Talika family has been stable is the absence of communalism in the village. The extended family is the basic economic unit in Talika, and each family occupies a specific sector of the seashore, where the large canoes are pulled upon land, and where family members gather together, some repairing nets, others preparing to enter the sea. The location of the family is determined by status. The higher the status, the closer to the village. The *oba*'s family, as expected, occupies the most convenient position.

The importance of the family in Talika is reflected in the realm of social control. If a young man wants to travel outside the village, it is proper etiquette for him to inform the *oba*, but it is his father's permission that counts. In Olowo it is just the opposite. Without the permission of the *oba* a person cannot travel. In such matters his father is without authority, although this situation may be on the verge of changing.

Marriage

Polygyny has existed in Talika since the village was founded. As in Olowo in 1970, the number of wives a man has varies with his status. In Table 8.1 it is

---

[1]The union of Olowo and Talika is described in detail in Chapter 8 of my Ph.D. thesis (Barrett, 1971).

TABLE 8.1. NUMBER OF WIVES PER MAN IN TALIKA

category	no. of men in category	average no. of wives
all married men in sample	48	2.2
prophets	8	4
landlords (including the eight prophets)	20	3.5
landlords (excluding the eight prophets)	12	3
town guards	5	3
all married men over 40 not prophet or town guard	9	2.9
all married men under 40 not prophet or town guard	26	1.4

shown that the average number of wives for all married men in a sample of 50% of the male population is 2.2.[2] The prophets, who enjoy the highest status, have an average of four wives each. The town guards enjoy more prestige than average, and they have three wives each, as do those landlords who are not prophets. The number of wives a man has also varies with his age. In a sample of all married men over 40 who are not prophets or town guards, the average number of wives is 2.9. In a sample of men under 40 of the same status, the average is 1.4 wives.

As in Olowo, there is no actual marriage ceremony. Instead, the *oba* simply announces publicly the union of the parties involved. Differences do exist, however. For example, the Talika leader does not choose a person's marriage partner. This is the prerogative of the parties involved and their families. Further, the *oba* does not manipulate the stratification system by determining the number of wives his subjects can have. Nor does he distribute women among men whom he wishes to reward. Instead the number of wives a man has is a function of economic well-being and personal preference.

This must be qualified. The *oba* has eight wives, more than any other man in Talika. This could be a result of his economic position, for he is a hard worker, and his sons are accomplished fishermen. However, informants state that he is only the second most wealthy man in the village. The lesser number of wives possessed by this other man may simply be a result of his own preference. But I suspect that it also has to do with status: nobody should have as many wives as the *oba*.

---

[2]All the figures in this chapter are derived from a questionnaire administered to the samples of the male and female sectors that are described in footnote 9, Chapter 1.

Another difference concerns bride price. Except in the case of women who join Olowo, no bride price is paid in the village. In Talika there is a bride price, which is said to be 25 pounds in all cases. Its absence in Olowo is accounted for by the communal system, under which members do not pay for goods and services. Given the major economic and family changes in Olowo, the appearance of a bride price is a further potential change in the future.

Finally, there was no indication that divorce had been rampant in Talika as in Olowo. The divorce rate was determined by data collected for a sample of 36 married women. In contrast to the 91% of Olowo women who changed husbands in 1966 alone, only 16.6% of the Talika women have been divorced since the village was founded. As in Olowo, divorce is normally accompanied by remarriage. Thus the number of women now married is equal to the sum of those divorced and not divorced.

I now want to consider conflict. It was shown that the competition for wives and sexual partners is a major source of strain in Olowo. Inasmuch as marriage and the family have been stable in Talika, it may be assumed that conflict will have been minimal.

Again it is necessary to distinguish between external and internal conflict. Relative to the external, it is important also to emphasize once more that Talika is much less of a closed community than Olowo. In the latter village people have almost no interaction with their relatives who live in surrounding communities. In contrast, a feature that quickly impressed me in Talika was that interaction with relatives in nearby villages is widespread and legitimate. For example, one day I accompanied a young Talika man to a village where his father's elder sister lived. As I learned, he is a constant visitor to her house. Moreover she was providing support for his education.

While interaction between family members in and out of the village seems to be widespread and harmonious, there is a major source of strain between Talika and its neighbors. This concerns marriage. As in the case of Olowo, there is bitterness as a result of the recruitment of outside women as members. For instance, in early 1970 a major celebration was held at Talika. As part of the festivities a dance was organized, and neighboring villagers were invited. An old man in one of the villages warned his daughter not to attend, but when he went fishing she disobeyed him. On his return he discovered what had happened and headed for Talika. When he demanded to see his daughter, nobody helped him, but eventually he spotted her among those dancing. He caught hold of her and began to beat her, but was restrained by members of Talika. He then was taken forcefully to the *oba,* who ordered his release. As soon as this was done the old man unexpectedly attacked the *oba,* ripping his robe before being pulled off.

The members of Talika were enraged. They knocked the old man down and beat him with their fists. They then dragged him away from the palace to an open space. There they stripped him naked, stuck four stakes into the ground, and tied his arms and legs to the stakes with rope. By this time sticks had been brought and several young men took turns beating him. This continued for over an hour. Finally, the *oba* sent word that they should stop. The incident had happened about 8 p.m., and it was not until after midnight that the old man was released. He then returned quietly to his own village, but without his daughter.

Members of Talika said this was not the first time the old man had caused trouble in the village. The reason was always the same: he feared his daughters would be seduced by Talika youth, and perhaps be persuaded to become members. Talika people said that the old man was of high status in his own village, and had two well-educated sons. But they insisted he was a heavy drinker, and that it was only because he was drunk that he had come to cause trouble. I do not know if he was drunk or not. It was dark, the commotion was great, and he was tied in the long grass. Consequently the only impressions I had were his anger and his suffering.

Although the recruitment of women is a major source of conflict between Talika and its neighbors, it is my impression that the hostility is not as extreme as in Olowo. This is because of the lesser social gap between Talika and the outside world; and perhaps because of its lack of economic success, which makes it a less visible target.

The major source of internal conflict in Olowo is adultery. In Talika there are two main sources: adultery and witchcraft.[3] Witches live in Olowo as well, but they are said to be less numerous than in Talika. The two sources are not unrelated. The people of Talika believe that female witches are much more prevalent than male witches; and they believe that adultery is often caused by the evil influence of witches. For example, one night the *oba* had a vision that a nonmember who worked in the village had seduced his wives. During the church service the next morning, the *oba* sent a message for this man to come to the church. When he entered he was slapped by the *oba,* who then accused him of adultery. The outsider pleaded innocence and finally was released. After the service was over the nonmember accused the witches of being responsible for his misfortune. He said they delight in causing trouble for strangers. This person is a Moslem. He immediately began three days of fasting.

As in Olowo, marriage fidelity is a major value. The *oba,* the other prophets, and the town guards spend much of their time making sure this ideal is not violated. In one case, a young man was suspected of sleeping with a married woman. One night members of the town guard crept into his room. The young man had heard them coming and his companion managed to escape out a window onto the verandah, and from there to her own house in the women's sector. However, the guards were not easily dissuaded. They brought the case to the attention of the prophets, who heard it one afternoon in the church. Present were

---

[3] Witchcraft beliefs in Talika are described in Chapter 3 of my Ph.D . thesis (Barrett, 1971).

the prophets, the town guards, the young man, the girl and the outraged husband. As it materialized, there was not enough evidence to prove their guilt. Nevertheless, the husband, who was a new recruit to the village, accused the young man of being a rascal and a poor Christian. The latter in turn accused him of being a pagan until recently, only briefly introduced to true Christianity, and hence in no position to accuse a long-standing member of behavior unbecoming to a Christian.

Had the girl and the young man been proved guilty, punishment would have been severe. Both would have been flogged, and perhaps assigned a piece of work. Some informants added that at times the guilty would be stripped naked and led around the village, but I observed no cases of this.

In summary, in spite of the relative stability of marriage and the family in Talika, and the lesser social distance between it and the outside world, competition for women is a major source of conflict. The difference between Olowo and Talika is a matter of degree. In the latter village, neither external nor internal conflict generated by relations between men and women appears to be as severe.

Residence

As in Olowo, Talika is divided into male and female sectors, so that husband and wife do not live together. Similarly, young children of both sexes are raised in the female sector, and at the age of five or six the boys move across to the male sector. In an earlier chapter it was explained why Olowo is divided in this manner. Members of the village said that it was a result of nonsocial factors: the odor of fish, the smoke from processing them, and the threat of fire in the house, where the fish previously were processed. I suggested that while nonsocial factors were important, social factors could not be ignored. Splitting the village into two sectors diminished the rivalry of the family with the communal social organization.

A consideration of the Talika case would seem to affirm the argument of members of Olowo that nonsocial rather than social factors were responsible for the unique residence pattern. Talika is not organized along communal lines. Thus the division of the village must be a result of some other factor or factors. The Talika people offered two explanations. The first was the same as that provided by Olowo members: the odor of the fish, the smoke, and the threat of fire. The second involved a combination of religious and status factors. They stated that the sea had great religious significance, and they also argued that men were superior to women. The men, therefore, should be closer to the deity. Hence the division of the village into two sectors, with the women to the interior.

It is correct that the sea does have religious significance in Talika. For example, illness, which is attributed to spiritual factors, is often treated by submerging the

TABLE 8.2. NUMBER OF HOUSES
WITH AT LEAST TWO PEOPLE
RELATED BY KINSHIP

	male	female
relatives	20	20
no relatives	0	0
TOTAL	20	20

sick person in the sea. As well, one of the names in the *oba*'s title is *Okun,* the Yoruba word for "sea." I tried to discover if the sea had the same significance in Olowo, but this was denied by all my informants. Yet the Talika beliefs as regard the sea are not atypical, for the main deity in traditional Ilaje religion is *Malokun,* the god of the sea, and among the Aladuras in general water is used for healing purposes.

Because the nonsocial explanation was offered in both villages, it must be assumed to have some validity. I suppose it even could be argued that two different structures—communalism and religion—provided the same function in the two villages. But this is unconvincing, and I must admit that I cannot confidently explain why the two villages share this unique residential pattern. Finally, there is an alternative explanation that may be obvious, but appears to be wrong, and for this reason must be considered: the Talika people may simply have copied the innovation from Olowo, carrying the idea with them when they founded their own village. This is unlikely, for the leader of Talika and those loyal to him left Olowo in 1951, and the division into two sectors in Olowo did not occur until 1953. Because of the hostility between the two villages until 1969, it is improbable that Talika people would have imitated Olowo sometime after 1953.

Olowo and Talika, then, share this unique residence pattern. This, however, is the extent of the similarity. There is no kindergarten in Talika, and children there are raised by their own parents of the same sex even after they become 5 or 6 years old. More significant, while male and female are divided into two sectors, relatives of the same sex are not encouraged to live in different houses. Indeed the contrary prevails, as demonstrated in Table 8.2: in contrast to Olowo, every house in both sectors contains relatives.

The difference between the two communities is even greater than indicated in this table. Table 8.3 shows the number of people in the 20 houses in each sector that are related to each other. Everybody in the female sector is related to at least one other person in the house. Only one person in the male sector is not related to someone else. This man is a newcomer to Talika, having joined only in 1967. These findings contrast sharply with Olowo, especially with respect to the male sector. There only five of 14 houses in the sample contained relatives (see Tables 6.4 and 6.5). In further contrast to Talika, even in the houses with relatives not everybody was related to at least one other person. This was the case in both the male and female sectors.

TABLE 8.3. NUMBER OF PEOPLE
RELATED TO AT LEAST ONE
OTHER PERSON IN THE SAME
HOUSE

	male	*female*
related	174	96
not related	1	0
TOTAL	175	96

Table 8.4 summarizes the kinship connections of the 155 residents in the male sector to the 20 landlords. The majority are sons of the landlord. Except for seven people (the newcomer to Talika, the two unknown, and a man and his three sons) everyone is related to the landlord in some way. Table 8.5 presents the same material for the female sector. Again the majority are children of the landlady, including not only girls but also boys under the age of seven. An interesting case because it is exceptional is that of the co-wife of one landlady. In the entire sample only in this one case did two wives of one man live in the same house.

A further major difference between Olowo and Talika will now be considered. It was shown that residential lines in Olowo are not organized upon a kinship basis. Informants in Talika had suggested that their village was different. In order to examine this possibility, three lines in the female sector were selected.[4] In line A there are three houses. The landladies of two of them have the same husband. Nobody in the third house is related to anyone in the other two.

TABLE 8.4. RELATIONSHIP OF 155
RESIDENTS OF MALE SECTOR
TO 20 LANDLORDS

son	124
brother	9
son of brother living in house	5
son of brother not living in house	2
son of son	5
son of former husband of wife	3
not a relative of landlord	4
not a relative of anybody	1
unknown	2
TOTAL	155

---

[4] Almost all the houses in the male sector faced the main street, rather than being arranged in lines or side streets. Thus the project could not be repeated there.

TABLE 8.5. RELATIONSHIP OF 76
RESIDENTS OF FEMALE SECTOR
TO 20 LANDLADIES

daughter of landlady	50
son of landlady	14
sister of landlady	1
co-wife of landlady	1
daughter of daughter of landlady who lives in same house	4
wife of landlady's son	1
daughter of wife of landlady's son	1
daughter of co-wife of landlady living in same house	3
son of co-wife of landlady living in same house	1
TOTAL	76

In line B there are six houses. Two different pairs of landladies are co-wives of the same husband. The fifth landlady is the wife of the son of one of the four previous landladies. The sixth landlady is married to the brother of the husband shared by two of the landladies in the line. In this line, then, every house contains at least one person related to someone in another house in the same line.

Line C has seven houses. Three different pairs of the seven landladies share the same husband. In the other house nobody is related to anyone else in the line. In this case the landlady is a new member. She joined the community shortly after the third wife of one of the husbands married to one of the three pairs of landladies had died. The newcomer was allowed to move into her house.

Of the 16 houses in the three lines, 14 contain at least one person related to someone in another house in the same line. In contrast to Olowo, then, not only do relatives in Talika tend to live in the same house, but also in the same line.

In summary, while Olowo and Talika both share the innovation of separate male and female sectors, they are different in all other respects of residence patterns. First, in Talika no person lives in a house without at least one relative; indeed, in most cases everyone in the house is related in some way to everybody else. Second, it is probable that girls will be brought up in the same house as their mothers, and that boys over six will move to their fathers' houses in the male sector. Third, it is probable that every house in the line will have some kinship connection with at least one other house in the line.

Consequences of Union with Olowo

The Talika family has persisted as a stable and viable institution despite the fact that the village became a branch of Olowo in 1969. It was the understanding between the leaders of the two villages that the adoption of a communal social organization was a condition of the acceptance of Talika as a branch member. Had this occurred the family would have been weakened. It is important to emphasize, therefore, that it did not happen. The structure of the economy was not modified, and private enterprise continued as before. The structure of the family remained the same, with polygny the dominant marital form; and the family continued as the principal economic unit of the village.

Indeed, rather than being weakened, the family appears to have strengthened after the union with Olowo. This was a direct response to efforts by the leaders of both villages to persuade the Talika people to accept the communal system. As Talika members stressed, opposition to the communal system came mainly from the family. People were unwilling to trust the community to look after their welfare. Further, some families were much wealthier than others. They resented turning their possessions over to the community.

Although Olowo and Talika people say they are now one, the leaders of both villages have prohibited inter-village marriages. They have stated that in a few years such marriages would be legitimate but that so far it has been too early. The main reason for this, I think, is conflict. As has been shown, a major source of internal conflict in both villages has to do with male-female relations. The leaders are perfectly aware of this, and are reluctant to risk straining the union by permitting intermarriage. It is also possible that intermarriage has not been allowed because the leaders have some doubts as to whether the union will persist. Given such doubts, it is logical not to give away one's women.

In spite of the policy set by the leaders, there has been considerable informal contact among members of the opposite sex of the two villages. For example, a friendship began between a young bachelor from Talika and a married woman from Olowo. He visited her in her house whenever he came to Olowo. She in turn always prepared him meals. While many Olowo people were aware of their friendship, nobody tried to stop them from seeing each other. However, the landlady of the girl repeatedly warned them not to have sexual intercourse. They both agreed that it would be wrong to do so.

At one point the young man got into trouble in Talika as a result of unrelated factors, and decided to leave the village. The Olowo girl found out what was happening, and was determined to leave her husband and run away with her friend. At this juncture, other people became concerned about the consequences that this might have for the union of the villages, and persuaded the lovers to remain in their own communities.

The apprehension in the two villages with regard to male-female relations is reflected in another case. During a church service in Talika, a man was accused of arranging a liaison between an Olowo girl and a Talika youth. The case was dismissed because of a lack of evidence, but for a while the situation was very tense. This was because it involved a member of Olowo. In dismissing the case, the *oba* warned his subjects not to let Olowo people know about it, since it could lead to tension between the two villages.

Incest

The structure and function of marriage and the family has been stable since Talika was founded. This includes the period after union with Olowo. However, one significant change has recently occurred. It concerns the incest taboo. Around 1968, the *oba* decided upon a new marriage policy: brother and sister should be preferential marriage partners.

It should be stressed that an incest taboo is well-rooted in Ilaje society. Indeed, in the traditional villages when a marriage is planned the elders will first trace the genealogy of each party. If any blood tie can be established within the last eight generations, the relationship is considered incestuous, and the marriage is not allowed.

I am not sure whether siblings who share the same parents are to marry, or only brother and sister who have one of their parents in common. Informants were inclined to say it was the latter. It was not possible to examine a number of incestuous marriages in order to establish a pattern, because only one union of brother and sister had so far taken place. In this case a daughter and son of different wives of the *oba* were forced by their father to marry. Informants say that the son was willing, but that the daughter was reluctant. She apparently fled from the village, but was caught a couple of days later and forced to consummate the marriage with her brother.

While this is the only incestuous union to date, the *oba* insists it will be the trend in the future, and is adamant that all his own children will intermarry. Among his subjects, the younger people are opposed to the new marriage policy. One reliable informant said that only the most backward and uncivilized of them can accept it. Anybody with any education, he remarked, would reject it as wicked. This same young man said it is quite likely that all the *oba*'s children will intermarry because they are the most backward in the village. The *oba* has not allowed them to become well-educated, and rarely lets them leave the village. For these reasons, the informant stated, the children of the *oba* do not know any better.

The elders publicly support the *oba*. However, none has tried to force his own children to marry one another. They have not made any attempt, according to the youth, because they realize their children would escape from the village rather than submit.

It is of interest that signs of similar behavior recently emerged in Olowo. During a church service in 1970 the *oba* told his subjects that that they were wrong to think marriage between relatives is sinful. He said that in future they would marry even their close relatives, but not brother or sister. He anticipated the reaction of his subjects by accusing them of being conservative.

Why has there been an attempt to remove the incest taboo? In Talika the answer lies mainly with the *oba*, for it was his idea that brother and sister should marry. He said that the deity told him in a dream that he should introduce this policy, and justifies his action by referring to the Bible. This explanation must be taken seriously, for in contrast to the practice in Olowo, dreams and visions in Talika demand concrete action in the real world.

A more analytical interpretation of the phenomenon could focus upon the nature of authority in the village. Talika is a religious community. The prophets have the greatest status and authority, and the *oba* is supposedly the most powerful prophet of all. In order to demonstrate his worth in office, he must constantly reveal signs of his power. Visions are one way of achieving this end.

Olowo requires a different explanation. The main reason for encouraging marriage between relatives seems to be the shortage of women. The recent trend toward polygyny has been accompanied by an energetic recruitment of outside women. However, it is still necessary for young men to wait until they are almost 30 before they are given a wife. The young men complain. During a church service the *oba* told them to be patient, remarking that if they were desperate they could arrange to meet their mothers. While this remark was greeted with laughter, his further remark that Olowo people would soon begin to marry their relatives was received more soberly. In reality, the removal of the incest taboo would not increase the overall number of marriagable people. But the change in policy still may be important: we have seen that the higher a man's status, the more wives he has, and the more likely he will receive a gift from the *oba*, such as a radio or a wife. The effect of removing the incest taboo is to widen the range of eligible partners. This would make it easier for the *oba* to increase the flow of women to high-status people, and decrease it to low status people. Such a policy would fit the *oba*'s decision that important people should be highly rewarded.

A less convincing explanation of the weakening of the incest taboo in Olowo is that the *oba* knew of the plan in Talika to have brother and sister marry. The remarks of the Olowo leader in the church were made a few months after the union with Talika. It is possible that he copied the Talika policy, only to a lesser degree. If this is the case, it is one of the rare instances in which Talika has influenced Olowo, rather than the reverse.

To conclude, the Talika family has never been suppressed. The only major change has been the effort to remove the incest taboo. This is more in the mind of the *oba* than a reality. At any rate it is not even remotely significant for the relationship between family type and industrialization, which is the focus of discussion in the next chapter.

9. Discussion: Olowo and Talika

An important part of modernization theory concerns the relation between family type and economic development. The literature addressed to this relationship contains two major propositions:

1. The emergence of the nuclear family is a necessary consequence of industrialization.
2. The extended family retards industrialization.

The better fit of the nuclear family to development is said to rest on its potential to perform two specific functions: it facilitates geographical mobility and it reduces ascription in the work sphere. Both functions in turn rest on assumptions that are intrinsic to modernization theory. One is that in an industrial society people must be prepared to relocate where work is available. The nuclear family is said to make this more possible because kinship ties outside the immediate family are weakened, and hence have less hold on the individual. The other is that in an industrial society both the level of technology and the constant movement of the labor force require that universalistic standards operate in order that qualified personnel are recruited. Recruitment on the basis of family connection presumably would destroy a technologically-based society.

The two major propositions are well-established in the literature. What I intend to do is to demonstrate that they are without empirical foundation. The evidence is twofold. First, it will be shown that the recent trend in the literature challenges the propositions. Second, it will be shown that Olowo and Talika both support this trend.

The Literature

The growing skepticism with regard to the two general propositions is summed up by Singer (1968, p. 423):

Although treated as axiomatic in many sociology textbooks, this theory has been challenged during the last fifteen years from three different directions: the documentation by social anthropologists of the variety of family systems in different parts of the world; the discovery by social historians that the nuclear family may have been prevalent and a cultural norm in Europe and United States even before industrialization; and the finding by sociologists and social anthropologists that many families in American and European cities maintain widespread kin ties.

A number of scholars have challenged the proposition that nuclearity is a consequence of industrialization. In an influential study based in London, for example, Young and Willmott (1967) discovered that the extended family was very much alive. In another London study Marris arrived at the same conclusion. As he states (1967, p. 40): "After one hundred and fifty years of an industrial society, the people of Bethnal Green still seemed . . . to belong to widespread, cohesive kin groups . . ." Referring to French Canada and Japan, Greenfield (1961–1962) argues that urbanization and industrialization can take place without the nuclear family. Johnson (1964) also points to Japan as a case in which the nuclear family has not emerged. But as he indicates, both Dore and Smith have reported two distinct urban family patterns in Japan. One is the "downtown pattern" in which the stem family is dominant. The second is the "fringe" type which is found in the suburbs, and approximates to the Western type of nuclear family. Even in Russia, where the family was supposed to wither away, Geiger (1968, p. 176) observes that the extended family has persisted in cities.

Moore fluctuates between arguing that nuclearity is a necessary consequence of economic development and that it is by no means inevitable. He says that mobility—both geographical and social—is a requisite for economic growth (1965, p. 86), and ". . . has negative consequences for extended family systems and tends to reduce the close ties between adult generations and adult siblings." (1963, p. 102). But Moore qualifies this by stating: "Although some scholars have taken the view that only the small-family system is possible in industrial societies, this generalization is too sweeping. The social responsibilities to kinsmen beyond the 'nuclear' family of parents and their immature offspring become weak and permissive rather than obligatory, but may endure." (1963, p. 102).

Goode (1964 and 1966) adopts a position akin to Moore's. He admits that the conjugal family is emerging in most societies undergoing industrialization. But he also stresses that all recent studies in Great Britain and U.S. show widespread contact among relatives. He concludes that while both the family and industrialization influence each other, neither fully determines the other. Finally, in an article entitled "The Isolated Nuclear Family: Fact or Fiction," with special reference to United States, Sussman (1959) concludes that it is mostly fiction—that ties with kin are widespread.

All these studies deal with complex societies. But the same trend is found in studies that concern developing countries. LeVine (1963), for example, refers to Bradburn's findings that in Turkey the patrilocal family sometimes is maintained in apartment buildings, with married sons living in apartments in the same buildings as their parents. Beteille and Singer report similar findings for India. The former (1964) finds very little difference between family types in rural and urban areas. Reporting on Madras City, Singer (1968, p. 444) states: ". . . the urban and industrial members of a family maintain numerous ties and obligations with the family members who have remained in the ancestral village or town or have moved elsewhere. And within the urban and industrial setting a modified joint family organization is emerging. The metropolitan industrial center has simply become a new arena for the working of the joint family system." Finally, in a brief review of the literature on West Africa, Aldous (1965) concludes that it is erroneous to assume that the extended family is disappearing. My own impressions among the Ibo in cities such as Enugu strongly support this conclusion.

The proposition that the nuclear family necessarily follows upon industrialization appears unsatisfactory from yet another point of view. In a review of 26 studies of the joint family in India, Kolenda (1968) stresses that there is little agreement about what constitutes the joint family. This diversity is also emphasized by Beteille. He observes that those who assume that the nuclear family is a consequence of development fail to take into account the great variety of family forms that existed prior to development. Beteille stresses as well that the family is not static, and refers to Goody's (1958) theory of the developmental cycle of domestic groups to emphasize his point. The implication is that because of the ambiguity of what constitutes the joint family and the fact that the family varies over time, it cannot be confidently assumed that the nuclear family follows economic development.

While the evidence is thin and speculative, some writers have recently argued that the nuclear family may even be a prerequisite for economic development. The earlier quotation from Singer, for example, suggested that the nuclear family may have existed in Europe and U.S. before industrialization began. While stressing that no large-scale study has ever verified the assumption, Goode (1964) remarks that the nuclear family in some places may have predated industrialization, and thus be the independent variable. Greenfield (1961–1962) makes an identical claim, and argues that in Barbados the nuclear family exists now in the absence of development. As Johnson (1964) reports, Arensberg reinforces the argument relative to Europe; and Furstenberg (1966) contends that the presentday family in United States is much the same as it was in early colonial days.

It seems therefore, that the long-accepted proposition that the nuclear family is a consequence of development is in error. However, it would be wrong to leave the impression that the extended family in its classical form persists in industrial societies. Recent research has been more sensitive to the precise nature of the family. For example, in a paper describing family ties in industrial society, Firth (1964, p. 87) remarks:

The term "extended family" has often been used for the set of kin so involved. Like most other anthropologists I tend to use this term rather sparingly, to refer to groups of kin of three generations or more, having a fairly well defined corporate lineal character, such as co-operation in ordinary productive activities, common ownership of assets, recognized common responsibilities. Shared or contiguous residence is a usual but not necessary concomitant of extended family membership . . . For the relationships of the type described in this paper I prefer to use a term such as "close kin unit" or "set."

In his later extensive study of the family in London, Firth (1969) suggests that a distinction be made between the extended family and extrafamilial kin. He defines the first as a type in which authority usually resides in the senior male, who rules over the various nuclear families that constitute the extended family. He defines the second as a type in which authority is dispersed among the various nuclear families. Firth argues that this latter type is more appropriate to describe family relations in London today. This type would appear to coincide with Moore's statement, in which he said that in complex societies kin ties become weakened but still endure.

In a lively reaction to Firth's earlier paper, Townsend argues that the conclusion that the elementary or nuclear family emerges with industrialization, even if some extrafamily ties remain, is not supported by the evidence. As Townsend states (1964, p. 92): "The extended family is indeed *the* primary group for a substantial proportion . . . of the populations of industrial societies."

The problem here appears to be one of definition. Townsend (1964, p. 92) defines the extended family as: ". . . the group of from 3 to 20 or more relatives who are in daily or almost daily contact and who include at least two individuals who stand in a relationship different from that of any two members of the *immediate* or *nuclear* family of parents and unmarried dependent children." Townsend seems to equate the "extended family" with what Firth means by "extra-familial kin." My own judgment is that Firth's concept is more precise, and represents what most authors who have been reviewed here mean by the extended family. If this is the case, the theoretical argument in this chapter is weakened, for we have in mind something quite different from the type of family organization assumed by those who in the past accepted the two major propositions. But the argument is not destroyed, because the evidence overwhelmingly rejects the assumption that the isolated nuclear family has emerged in most industrialized societies.

Recent studies also have quarreled with the proposition that the extended family retards development. A strong statement to the contrary has been made by Belshaw (1964, p. 221): "It is not necessary to turn a matrilineage into a patrilineage or to create a nuclear family before economic growth can take place, and to attempt to do so may delay the take-off for a considerable period of time."

In reference to India, Hoselitz, Beteille, and Singer all take a similar stance. Hoselitz (1961, pp. 111–112) argues that rather than being a handicap for development, the extended family makes it possible for an artisan wishing to expand his business to obtain funds, where regular bank credit is almost impossible to obtain. Goode makes a comparable claim for the extended family. He says it has the advantage of amassing capital for investment, and argues that the whole extended family can function as a sort of savings bank.

The two specific functions that supposedly are served by the nuclear but not the extended family also have come under attack. With respect to geographical mobility, Christopher (1965, p. 103) remarks: "It has become part of the folklore of sociology that the extended family hinders geographical mobility, that geographical mobility is a *sine qua non* for industrialization, and that therefore the extended family ties are an impediment to industrialization in the developing nations of Africa and Asia. Actual research, however, does not bear out the hypothesis."

One reason for doubting the contribution of geographical mobility is that it inevitably involves migration from rural to urban areas. Yet as Barber (1967, pp. 108–109) states, urbanization can be parasitic in developing societies. It does not necessarily lead to industrialization. It simply means the transfer of unemployed and poor people from the countryside to the town. In accord with Barber's argument, Hauser (1966, p. 205) suggests that in developing nations programs should be devised for keeping people in rural areas, in order to concentrate on agriculture.

Even in industrial societies, extensive geographical mobility is not necessarily correlated with nuclearity. Both Litwak (1960a) and Sussman (1959), for example, found that in U.S. there still is considerable contact among relatives. Both explain this by suggesting that in spite of geographical mobility, modern transportation allows relatives to keep in contact. The same argument is made for West Africa by Comhaire (1965).

Elsewhere Litwak (1960b) observes that Parsons and others are correct in saying that the extended family is negative for an industrial society. But this only holds for the period of "emerging industrialization." Litwak makes a distinction between "emerging" and "mature" industrialization, and between the "classical" and a "modified" extended family. By modified, he means a series of nuclear families bound loosely together. His argument is that in the early stages of industrialization the classical extended family does impede development, but in the mature stage, the modified extended family is of great aid, especially for the upwardly mobile young nuclear family which receives the support of the extended family. It is relevant to add that in a study done on family relations in Montreal, Osterreich (1965) found it useful to employ Litwak's concept of the modified extended family to classify her material.

Finally, both Sussman and Hubert have commented on the degree of aid given to relatives in industrial societies, but have not arrived at the same conclusion. In a study based in United States, Sussman found that aid to relatives is more frequent among middle than among lower-class families. In a study of migrants to London, Hubert (1965) found the opposite. Her explanation is that the middle class do not *require* the aid of relatives. Unlike lower-class migrants who search for a job *after* moving to the city, middle-class migrants usually have a job arranged *before* they move to the city. Discrepancies in findings such as these are not to be interpreted negatively. They are signs of a growing sensitivity with respect to the precise nature of family relations in complex societies, rather than to a confusing stereotype of these relations.

The second specific function of the nuclear family concerns the anticipated change from ascribed to achieved criteria as a basis of recruitment and reward in the economic sphere. As was explained, this transformation is assumed to take place by virtue of the greater mobility of the nuclear family, and of the consequent reduction in kinship obligations beyond the immediate family. Yet Lloyd (1969, pp. 95 and 107), Little (1965), Mayer (1961), and Wilson and Mafeje (1963) have argued that migration to towns does not diminish kinship ties. Indeed, it may intensify not only family ties but also tribal ties. What this means is that the degree of universalism is even less than before migration took place.

This in itself is not inimical to economic development. Indeed, Cohen (1969) has shown in a Hausa migrant community in Ibadan that there is a direct correlation between the strength of ethnic ties and economic success. Cohen's work constitutes an enormous blow to the sociological tradition that rests on typologies such as Parsons' pattern-variables (1951, p. 67). Such criticism is long overdue. Only armchair theorists can continue to assume that the distinction between industrial and non-industrial societies suggested by such a typology is relevant to either case.

To summarize, two propositions have for long been accepted in the literature relating family type to industrialization. Recent investigators, however, have challenged both of them. Of special significance is the more precise conceptualization of the phenomenon, as reflected in the works of Firth and Litwak. Firth's concept of extrafamilial kin is similar to Litwak's concept of the modified extended family. Both concepts suggest the continued interaction of kin in industrial society, without assuming that family relations in complex and simpler societies are identical.

Olowo and Talika

It will now be shown that Olowo and Talika support this recent trend in the literature. Two assumptions can be made about the relation of family type to economic development in Olowo. The first is that the nuclear family did not emerge after the village industrialized. The only conflicting evidence concerns the reign of the first *oba*. Most men then had only one wife, except when marriage was banned. This was not, however, because monogamy was the ideal, but because of the shortage of women and the ideal of equality. Further, although most men had only one wife, this was not associated with a close-knit unit consisting of parents and offspring. Husband and wife did not live together, and usually their children lived with other adults. Nor was a person's primary allegiance to the family. Instead it was to the community.

Even if the nuclear family had emerged in Olowo during the early part of reign I, it would be unreasonable to attribute it to the village's industrialization, for the influence of industrialization on the family would not be felt so quickly. In this context the changes in the family during the reign of the third *oba* have more significance. As shown quantitatively in Chapter 6 (see Tables 6.2 and 6.3), there was a sharp increase in polygyny after 1966. This was *after* the village had rapidly industrialized. It is tempting to argue that not only has polygyny increased but also that the extended family has become stronger. My evidence for this, however, consists only of my personal impressions. Part of it concerns the tendency for relatives to pool their resources in order to purchase canoes, and thus accumulate income for the family.

Further evidence was provided by informants in relation to residence patterns. They said that the change in residence could not be measured accurately by looking only at the proportion of children living with either parent. This is because of a recent tendency for a child of six or more to move to a house of a relative, such as father's brother, if not to the father's house itself. Some support for their argument was found, but I do not know if the pattern is any different than in the past. An identical problem exists as regards the amount of visiting among relatives, which I observed to be widespread in 1970.

Polygyny, therefore, increased after the village industrialized, and it is probable that the extended family has emerged as a viable unit. This is in the classical sense; the concepts of extrafamilial kin and the modified extended family are not applicable to Olowo. The implication is clear: the Olowo case solidly rejects the long-accepted proposition that nuclearity follows development.

The second assumption is that the rapid economic development of Olowo was partly a consequence of its family organization. This assumption was considered in Chapter 3, but is restated here because of its significance for the body of theory now being examined. My argument is that the weakened family did not interfere with the communal system, therefore permitting the latter's potential contribution to the village's economic expansion to be realized. The assumption that the communal system and the family are incompatible is supported by Talmon-Garber (1962, p. 469) in reference to the kibbutz: "Deep attachment to the family may weaken the primary group characteristics of the kibbutz and disrupt its unity. The families may tend to become competing foci of intensive emotional involvement and to infringe upon devotion to the community."

Finally, the two established propositions will be considered once more. The Olowo family was suppressed until recently. It could be argued that it was suspended in time, and that the increase in polygyny and the renewed strength of the extended family have emerged because of a necessity to go through this stage of family organization. The implication is that it is only a question of time before the nuclear family appears, for its absence is simply a result of the earlier family suppression. Not much weight is attached to this argument, but it is offered as a remote possibility.

The second major proposition has been ignored in the discussion of Olowo, because the extended family was not a feature of the village. But given the recent legitimation of the extended family, it is now appropriate to ask whether further economic development will be retarded. The answer must be speculative, for the influence of the family is not likely to be measurable until at least a generation passes. What does seem clear is that the immediate consequences have been positive. As indicated earlier, family members are getting together to purchase boats, in order to increase their private income through fishing. Moreover, the potential reward of several wives for hard work is a significant source of motivation for the men. It is unlikely that the women in Olowo will rise against this inequality; therefore their motivation will be assured by their husbands. My guess, then, is that while Olowo may well fail to maintain its phenomenal rate of economic growth, such failure would not be attributable to revitalization of the extended family.

Three assumptions can be made about the relationship between family type and economic development in Talika. The first is that the extended family contributed positively to the economy during the village's early years.[1] It will be recalled that some authors such as Belshaw, Hoselitz, and Goode have argued that rather than being a negative factor, the extended family may well be beneficial by providing funds for economic enterprises. Talika is a case that supports this argument. Most Talika men are fishermen. This enterprise requires considerable funds in order to purchase canoes, motors, and nets. It also requires large labor units. In order to be productive, several people must be available to go to sea, mend nets, and process and market the fish. The latter work is done by women, who are therefore a major part of the work unit. The implication is that the extended family is a more appropriate structure than the nuclear family, given the nature of the major economic activity in Talika. It has the capacity to provide the prerequisites of both capital and labor. Only a combination of several nuclear families, or some other form of cooperation among a sufficient number of people (not necessarily kinsmen), could perform in the same manner.

The second assumption is that the extended family has ceased to contribute positively to development in Talika in recent years. How can it be defended, given the validity of the initial assumption? The change in function of the extended family is a consequence of an exogenous factor: fishing has deteriorated in the Ilaje area. The deterioration is in both absolute and relative terms. It is absolute inasmuch as Ilaje residents claim that the sea is no longer good; fish are not as plentiful as in the past. It is relative inasmuch as the revolution of rising expectations also has entered Ilaje. People desire bicycles, radios, etc. I have no way of knowing if fishing actually has become worse. However, even if it has not decreased in absolute terms, it is probable that dissatisfaction still would be widespread.

How is the extended family related to the deterioration of fishing? Fishing is a family-dominated activity in Talika. In the past this was positive inasmuch as both capital and labor were made available. The members of Talika no longer consider the fishing industry to be productive, but their reaction is to try to increase, or at least to maintain, the role of the extended family in the industry. Parents insist that their sons become fishermen, rather than leave the village to train as clerks or technicians. If a young man is reluctant to fish, he may have

---

[1] I have not forgotten that Talika has not developed economically. The assumption concerns the *potential* of a particular type of family to contribute to economic growth.

to leave the village against the will of his father. This unwillingness of parents to allow their sons to seek other employment is indicated by the fact that only a handful of members work on the two passenger launches owned by the community. Instead outsiders are hired to run them.

In other words, the energies of the people are channelled into an economic enterprise that is no longer seen as profitable. Unless Talika manages to obtain trawlers such as those in Olowo—an unlikely event—the probability of prosperity from fishing is minimal. This is an interesting case, then, in which a structural variable (the extended family) has been transformed from positive to negative, but in which a populace has not recognized (or accepted) the change.

The third assumption is that the emergence of the nuclear family in Talika would not contribute to economic growth. Given the argument that the extended family no longer contributes positively, the assumption would appear to be suspect. Yet it can be supported as follows. The only economic activity of note in the village is fishing. If the extended family was replaced by the nuclear family, what would be the consequences? A major one would be widespread migration to the mainland among the young men. One reason for this is that the nuclear family would be unsuitable for the fishing industry, so that there would be no reason to remain in the village. Such migration may be positive inasmuch as some of the young men may be fortunate enough to find alternative employment in factories, or to receive training as clerks, etc. However, it would be negative with respect to economic growth within Talika, because few if any of those to receive specialized training would return permanently to the village.

To conclude, two propositions until recently have dominated the sociological literature concerning the relationship between the family and industrialization. One is that development of the nuclear family is a necessary consequence of industrialization. The other is that the extended family retards development. The case of Olowo rejects the initial proposition. The case of Talika rejects the second one.

Given the significance of Olowo and Talika for the theory relating family type and economic development, why has it not been the central focus of the manuscript? One reason is that I have been working with only two cases, which provide an inadequate ground for disproving the propositions. The strongest claim that can be made is that these propositions are not fruitful in explaining the relationship between economic and family change in Olowo and Talika. Yet the significance of the two cases is greatly increased by virtue of their fit with the recent trend in the literature.

The limited importance of two cases is not the only reason for caution. A more damaging one is the degree to which they diverge from the conditions usually associated with the two conventional propositions. One condition concerns time: changes in family structure occur gradually over a period of several generations. A second condition concerns the unit of analysis: the literature usually is addressed to changes taking place in large nations, not in small isolated villages.

Olowo does not meet either of the conditions. In time, the nuclear family may eventually become dominant. The family has already emerged as an economic unit. If in the future even more responsibility is placed on the family, to the extent that fees for primary, secondary, and university education must be paid for by the family, then one might anticipate a decrease in polygyny for economic reasons alone. My own guess is that this will not happen in the near future, if at all. The social solidarity of the village that is created by the social distance from the outside world, together with the sheer physical proximity of relatives resulting from the limited geographical mobility, will nullify the economic consideration.

With regard to the unit of analysis, by economic development we mean a very special case: that taking place within a small community. For this reason conditions for development usually associated with family change such as extensive geographical mobility are not relevant for Olowo. Indeed, such mobility would have been dysfunctional. Had the well-trained technicians, administrators, and fishermen left Olowo to take up jobs elsewhere, there probably would be no community called Olowo today, let alone a highly industrialized one.

The implication is that research findings focused upon one small village cannot legitimately be argued to have significance for the two long-accepted propositions relating family and economic change. However, it was shown that some authors such as Barber and Hauser argue that geographical mobility is a negative rather than positive factor. It merely results in shifting poor people from the country to the city. In these terms, Olowo may have significance for rural development after all.

It is relevant to add that the specific function thought to be associated with geographical mobility—the replacement of particularistic by universalistic criteria—is characteristic of the village in spite of the lack of such mobility. For example, even now that the family has achieved some degree of legitimacy in Olowo, a son may not work on the same launch as his father. This is in order to make sure no special privileges are granted. As well, if a person becomes involved in serious trouble, such as adultery, the last people that he can ask to plead his case with the *oba* are his relatives. This element of universalism has been introduced by virtue of the past suppression of the family; the communal system, as Goode has remarked, thus constitutes a more effective method of reducing the ascriptive nature of the family than the mere transition from an extended to a nuclear family.

Talika too is an exceptional case, but in a different manner. It has no significance for the proposition that nuclearity is a consequence of development, because it has not enjoyed the same economic success as in Olowo. For the same reason the time variable is not relevant. Yet the fact that it is only one small village rather than a nation state may mean that the conclusion that it constitutes an exception to the established theory is not legitimate.

However, I again refer to the remarks of Hauser and Barber regarding the benefit of rural development, and to the argument of Hoselitz and others that the extended family can provide labor and capital. The implication is that while a few years ago Talika might have been considered too exceptional to have any relevance for modernization theory, this no longer is the case.

Finally, a brief comment on the comparative framework is in order. Throughout my research Talika was employed as a control case in order to try to discover how Olowo developed so rapidly. The logical procedure was to search for inconstants between the two villages; for as Moore (1963, p. 19) remarks, a constant cannot explain variation, such as the greater economic success of Olowo. While the comparative method is to the anthropologist what the laboratory experiment is to the physical scientist, one must be careful not to assume that all constants are insignificant and all inconstants significant for the explanation of a phenomenon such as economic growth.

For example, the religious beliefs of Olowo and Talika are essentially the same. Yet religion does have minor importance for Olowo's economic success, by virtue of its contribution to social control, and its capacity to provide legitimacy for hard work and for the goal of development. At the same time it was found that communalism—an inconstant between the two villages—was a necessary but not a sufficient cause of Olowo's rapid development. It was supported by a number of other variables, the absence of which would have meant that Olowo would not have industrialized.

This leads to the following remarks: the difference in family structure *by itself* does not explain even partially the greater economic growth of Olowo. Indeed, we may argue that the extended family in Talika had more capacity to contribute to development than the suppressed family of Olowo—or than the nuclear family, had it existed. In order to industrialize, there must exist some organizing apparatus of the populace. It is only when the absence of kinship ties in Olowo is combined with the presence of communalism that the suppression of the family has significance for Olowo's economic success. Even this does not necessarily lead to economic growth. In order for this to happen the latter must exist as a goal.

CONCLUSION

Three major problems have guided the discussion. The first concerns the relationship between the introduction of communalism and the suppression of the family. It was argued that the latter was a consequence of the former; it enabled the communal system to function more effectively. A further consequence was the emergence of family substitutes. But the line and the landlord, etc., were not founded for this purpose. Instead their functions expanded to fill the vacuum created by the suppression of the family.

The implications of the Olowo case for the assumption that the family is universal were considered. As was shown, until 1966 Olowo diverged from the criteria established by Murdock for both marriage and the family in the same way as the kibbutzim did. This leaves us with the same problem that Spiro confronted: either it must be concluded that family and marriage did not exist in Olowo (at least at certain periods), or the criteria must be modified. This problem is compounded by the distinction between the family as a structural-functional and as a psychological unit. In the latter sense it can be said that even when marriage was banned entirely, the family still existed in Olowo. This is especially the case if it is acceptable to argue, as Spiro does, that the close-knit nature of the entire community is comparable to that of a large extended family.

The concept of structural-functional itself is ambiguous. Given such factors as the division of the village into male and female sectors, the Olowo family clearly does not exist in a structural sense according to Murdock's criteria. But it has been shown that several structures began to provide family functions. Again there is a problem in interpretation. By virtue of the fulfillment of the functions that Murdock associates with the family, can it be concluded that a structure (or complex of structures) exists that can be called a family? This appears to be the interpretation eventually favored by Spiro (see especially 1954, pp. 845–846).

My own judgment is that this is not satisfactory. The four functions set out by Murdock are prerequisites for the persistence of any self-sufficient society. If they are discovered in Olowo and in the kibbutz to be performed outside the structure of the family, there is no logical reason to widen the concept of the family to accommodate them. Quite apart from the definitional problem, neither in the kibbutz nor in Olowo was the family removed completely. This may be interpreted as support for Murdock's thesis that it is impossible to supplant the family entirely. But I do not think this conclusion is warranted, especially as regards

Olowo, for no attempt was made to abolish the family entirely.

The second problem concerns the relationship between the introduction of capitalism and the legitimation of the family. Unlike the first problem, evidence that the economy was the independent variable was not clear-cut. For this reason it was more appropriate to subsume both changes within the concept of normalization. It suggests functional interdependence, not causal primacy. The changes in both economic and family organization mark a transition from communal to private interests in the village. The emergence of both changes at approximately the same time was not accidental. It is improbable that a strong family could exist with the degree of communalism that was characteristic of the village. It also is unlikely that private enterprise could flourish without a viable family organization. Both are manifestations of private versus collective interests. The implication of these remarks is clear: the major structural changes in the economy and the family, both at the beginning and since 1966, underline the systemic nature of social institutions.

The third problem concerns the significance of Olowo and Talika for the literature that relates family type to economic development. Olowo does not fit the proposition that nuclearity follows development. Talika does not fit the proposition that the extended family retards development. It was stressed that neither village meets all the conditions normally associated with these propositions. However, while remembering that "extra familial kin" is a more precise concept than the "extended family," the recent trend in the literature questions the entire logic behind the propositions. Olowo and Talika are compatible with this trend. For this reason they are significant for the body of theory.

In concluding, a question will be raised that has been implicit throughout the study. What accounts for the receptivity of the Olowo people to innovation? How can they absorb the major changes in economic and family organization? This problem has been considered elsewhere (Barrett, 1971, Chapter 10). One of my main conclusions was that innovation and status are closely related: the higher one's status, the more likely to be an innovator. As evidence, 18 out of 24 innovations that were analyzed were initiated by high status people.

This leads once more to the power structure of Olowo. It was explained earlier that power is highly centralized in the village. By virtue of its utopian nature and the traditional content of the position of *oba,* the actor playing the role has great authority. Thus, whenever the contradition of the village with its setting generated a structural change—such as the legitimation of the family—or whenever the *oba* himself decided to manipulate the social system—such as donating wives to high status people—he was able to persuade his subjects to cooperate.

A further problem concerns conflict. It was shown that competition for sexual partners generates an enormous degree of strain in Olowo. In spite of the efforts of the present *oba,* this remains the case at present. This strain is primarily internally induced. It is generated by the nature of social conditions within Olowo itself. Moreover, the consequence is not the reattainment of an equilibrium. Instead it is the emergence of a new structural form, as, for example, in the numerous experiments with the marriage system. This has negative implications for equilibrium theorists such as Parsons, who assume that change is exogenously generated and that the system tends to persist, if only in the sense of a "moving equilibrium" (1951).

The normalization factor does not negate this argument. It is correct that the specific pattern of family change is predetermined by normalization: it will approximate to that which prevails in the dominant setting. However, the influence of normalization is a recent phenomenon. It does not account for the numerous experiments that date back to the founding of the village.

Finally, I return again to the predictions made about family organization. With regard to Talika, it is thought that the extended family will remain intact. The only potential change concerns incest, but it is anticipated that the attempt to remove the incest taboo will be abandoned, for there is too much resistance among the Talika people to enable it to work.

Relative to Olowo, it is predicted that husband and wife and their offspring, regardless of status, will constitute a residential unit in the future. At the same time, the family will emerge as the basic economic unit, with parents responsible for their own welfare as well as their children's. When this happens, the family will become a more prominent focus of conflict. At the same time the economic realm will not be conditioned to the same extent as in the past by universalistic values. In spite of all these changes, my last prediction is that there will not be a decrease in the range of polygyny or the strength of the extended family. If anything, they will emerge more prominently.

BIBLIOGRAPHY

Aldous, J. 1965. Urbanization, the extended family, and kinship ties in West Africa. In *Africa: social problems of change and conflict,* ed. P.L. van den Berghe. New York and London: Chandler, pp. 107–116.

Ames, D. 1963. Wolof cooperative work groups. In *Continuity and change in African cultures,* eds. W. Bascom and M. Herskovits. Chicago, Ill., University of Chicago Press, pp. 224–237.

Ardener, S. 1953. The social and economic significance of the contribution club among a section of the Southern Ibo. *Nigerian Institute of Social and Economic Research,* pp. 128–142.

Barber, W. 1967. Urbanization and economic growth: The cases of two white settler territories. In *The city in modern Africa,* ed. H. Miner. London: Pall Mall Press, pp. 91–125.

Barrett, S. 1971. *God's Kingdom on Stilts.* Ph. D. dissertation, University of Sussex, 1971.

Barrett, S. 1972. Crisis and change in a West African utopia. In *Perspectives in modernization,* ed. E. Harvey. Toronto: University of Toronto Press, 1972.

Bascom, W. 1942. The principle of seniority in the social structure of the Yoruba. *American Anthropologist* 44: 37–46.

Bascom, W. 1952. The *esusu:* a credit institution of the Yoruba. *Journal of the Royal Anthropological Institute* 82.

Bascom, W. 1969. *The Yoruba of southwestern Nigeria.* New York: Holt, Rinehart, and Winston, 1969.

Belshaw, C. 1964. Social structure and culture values as related to economic growth. *International Social Science Journal* 16: 217–228.

Bennett, J. 1967. *Hutterian brethren.* Stanford, Cal.: Stanford University Press, 1967.

Beteille, A. 1964. Family and social change in India and other South Asian countries. *The Economic Weekly* 16: 237–244.

Christopher, S. 1965. A note on research relevant to the extended family and geographical mobility. In *Kinship and geographical mobility,* ed. R. Piddington. Leiden: E.J. Brill, pp. 183–184.

Cohen, A. 1969. *Custom and politics in urban Africa.* London: Routledge and Kegan Paul.

Comhaire, J. 1965. Economic change and the extended family. In *Africa: social problems of change and conflict,* ed. P.L. van den Berghe. New York and London: Chandler, pp. 117–127.

Durkheim, E. 1938. *The rules of sociological method.* Glencoe, Ill.: The Free Press.

Firth, R. 1964. Family and kinship in industrial society. In *The Sociological Review Monograph No. 8: The Development of Industrial Societies,* ed. P. Halmos. University of Keele, England, pp. 65–87.

Firth, R. 1969. *Families and their relatives.* London: Routledge and Kegan Paul.

Furstenberg, F. 1966. Industrialization and the American family: a look backward. *American Sociological Review* 31: 326–337.

Geiger, H. 1968. *The family in soviet Russia.* Cambridge, Mass: Harvard University Press.

Gluckman, M. 1963. *Order and rebellion in tribal Africa.* London: Cohen and West.

Gold, R.L. 1958. Roles in sociological field observations. *Social Forces* 36: 217–223.

Goode, W. 1964. *The family.* Englewood Cliffs, N.J.: Prentice-Hall.

Goode, W. 1966. Industrialization and family change. In *Industrialization and society,* eds. B. Hoselitz and W. Moore. Unesco-Mouton, pp. 237–255.

Goody, J. 1966. The fission of domestic groups among the Lo Dagaba. In *The developmental cycle of domestic groups*, ed. J. Goody. Cambridge: Cambridge University Press, pp. 53–61.

Gough, K. 1959. The Nayars and the definition of marriage. *Journal of the Royal Anthropological Institute* 89: 23–34.

Gouldner, A. 1954. Patterns of industrial bureaucracy. New York: Free Press.

Greenfield, S. 1961–1962. Industrialization and the family in sociological theory. *American Journal of Sociology* 67: 312–322.

Hauser, P. 1966. The social, economic, and technological problems of rapid urbanization. In *Industrialization and society*, eds. B. Hoselitz and W. Moore. Unesco-Mouton, pp. 119–217.

Hoselitz, B. 1961. Tradition and economic growth. In *Tradition, values, and socio-economic development*, eds. R. Braibanti and J. Spengler. Durham, N.C.: Duke University Commonwealth Studies Center, pp. 83–113.

Hubert, J., 1965. Kinship and geographical mobility in a sample from a London middle-class area. In *Kinship and geographical mobility*, ed. R. Piddington. Aeiden: E.J. Brill, pp. 61–80.

Irvine, E. 1952. Observations on the aims and methods of child-rearing in communal settlements in Israel. *Human Relations* 5: 247–275.

Johnson, E. 1964. The stem family and its extension in present day Japan. *American Anthropologist* 66: 839–851.

Johnson, S. 1966. *The history of the Yorubas*. London: Routledge and Kegan Paul.

Junker, B. H. 1960. *Field work*. Chicago, Ill.: University of Chicago Press.

Kolenda, P. 1968. Region, caste, and family structure: A Comparative study of the Indian "joint" family. In *Structure and change in Indian society*, eds. M. Yinger and B. Cohn. Chicago: Aldine Atherton, Inc., pp. 339–396.

LeVine, R. 1963. Political socialization and cultural change. In *Old societies and new states*, ed. C. Geertz. Glencoe, Ill.: Free Press, pp. 280–303.

LeVine, R. 1966. *Dreams and deeds*. Chicago, Ill.: University of Chicago Press, 1966.

Levy, M. 1952. *The structure of society*. Princeton, N.J. Princeton University Press.

Levy, M. and Fallers, L. 1959. The family: some comparative considerations. *American Anthropologist* 61: 647–651.

Linton, R. 1943. Nativistic movements. *American Anthropologist* 45: 230–240.

Little, K. 1957. The role of voluntary associations in West African urbanization. *American Anthropologist* 59: 579–596.

Little, K.1965. *West African urbanization*. Cambridge: Cambridge University Press.

Litwak, E. 1960a. Geographic mobility and extended family cohesion. *American Sociological Review* 25: 385–94.

Litwak, E. 1960b. Occupational mobility and extended family cohesion. *American Sociological Review* 25: 9–21.

Lloyd, P.C. 1954. The traditional political system of the Yoruba. *Southwestern Journal of Anthropology* 10: 366–384.

Lloyd, P.C. 1957. The Itsekiri. In *Ethnographic survey of Africa, Western Africa* 13. London: International African Institute, 1957.

Lloyd, P.C. 1960. Sacred kingship and government among the Yoruba. *Africa:* 221–237.

Lloyd, P.C. 1966. Agnatic and cognatic descent among the Yoruba. *Man* 1: 484–500.

Lloyd, P.C. 1968. Divorce among the Yoruba. *American Anthropologist* 70: 67–81.

Lloyd, P.C. 1969. *Africa in social change*. Baltimore, Md.: Penguin Books.

Lloyd, P.C. Kings in crisis. Unpublished paper, School of Social Studies, University of Sussex.

Marris, P. 1961. *Family and social change in an African city*. London: Routledge and Kegan Paul.

Marris, P. 1967. Motives and methods: reflections on a study in Lagos. In *The city in modern Africa*, ed. H. Miner. London: Pall Mall Press. pp. 39–54.

Mayer, P. 1961. *Townsmen or tribesmen*. Cape Town: Oxford University Press.

McClelland, D. 1967. *The achieving society*. Glencoe, Ill.: The Free Press.

McClelland, E. 1966–1967. The experiment in communal living at Aiyetoro. *Comparative Studies in Society and History* 9:14–28.

Mencher, J. 1965. The Nayars of South Malabar. In *Comparative family systems,* ed. M. Nimkoff. Boston: Houghton Mifflin, pp. 163–191.

Mogey, J. 1962. Introduction to Part 1: Changes in the Family. *International Social Science Journal* 14: 411–424.

Moore, W. 1963. *Social change.* Englewood Cliffs, N.J.: prentice-Hall.

Moore, W. 1965. *The impact of industry.* Englewood Cliffs, N. J.: Prentice-Hall.

Murdock, G. 1966. *Social structure.* Beverly Hills, Cal.: Benziger, Bruce & Glencoe.

Osterreich, H. 1965. Geographical mobility and kinship: a Canadian example. In *Kinship and geographical mobility,* ed. R. Piddington. Leiden: E.J. Brill, pp. 131–144.

Ottenberg, S. 1963. Ibo receptivity to change. In *Continuity and change in African cultures,* ed. W. Bascom and M. Herskovits. Chicago, Ill: University of Chicago Press, pp. 130–143.

Parsons, T. 1951. *The social system.* Beverly Hills, Cal.: Benziger Bruce & Glencoe.

Peel, J. 1968. *Aladura: a religious movement among the Yoruba.* New York and London: Oxford University Press.

Radcliffe-Brown, A.R. 1961. On the concept of function in social science. In *Structure and function in primitive society.* Chapter 9. London: Cohen and West, 1961.

Schwab, W. 1955. Kinship and lineage among the Yoruba. *Africa* 25: 352–373.

Silverman, S.S. 1966. An ethnographic approach to social stratification: prestige in a central Italian community. *American Anthropologist* 68: 899–921.

Singer, M., 1968. The Indian joint family in modern industry. In *Structure and change in Indian society,* eds. M. Yinger and B. Cohn. Chicago, Ill.: Aldine-Atherton, Inc., pp. 423–452.

Spiro, M. 1954. Is the family universal? *American Anthropologist* 56:839–846. Reprinted with an appendix written in 1958 in *A modern introduction to the family,* eds. N.W. Bell and E.F. Vogel. Glencoe, Ill.: The Free Press 1960: pp. 64-75.

Spiro, M., 1963. *Kibbutz.* New York: Schocken Books.

Sussman, M. 1959. The isolated nuclear family: fact or fiction. *Social Problems* 6: 333–340.

Talmon, Y., 1965. The family in a revolutionary movement—the case of the kibbutz in Israel. In *Comparative family systems,* ed. M.F. Nimkoff. Boston: Houghton Mifflin, pp. 259–286.

Talmon-Garber, Y. 1962. Social change and family structure. *International Social Science Journal* 14: 468–487.

Townsend, P. 1964. Family and kinship in industrial society. In *The Sociological Review Monograph No. 8: The Development of Industrial Societies,* ed. P. Halmos. University of Keele, England, 89–96.

Turner, H.W. 1967. *History of an African independent church, 1. the church of the Lord (Aladura).* New York and London: Oxford University Press.

Uchendu, V. 1965. *The Igbo of Southeast Nigeria.* New York: Holt, Rinehart and Winston.

Wallace, A. 1956. Revitalization movements. *American Anthropologist* 58: 264–281.

Weber, M. 1930. *The protestant ethic and the spirit of capitalism.* Trans. Talcott Parsons. New York: Charles Scribner's Sons.

Weber, M. 1965. *The theory of social and economic organization.* Glencoe, Ill.: The Free Press.

Weintraub, D. *et al.* 1969. *Moshava, kibbutz, and moshav.* Ithica & London: Cornell University Press.

Wilson, M. and Mafeje, A. 1963. *Langa.* Cape Town: Oxford University Press.

Worsley, P. 1970. *The trumpet shall sound.* England: Paladin.

Young, M. and Willmott, P. 1967. *Family and kinship in East London.* London: Routledge and Kegan Paul.

INDEX

113

DATE DUE

APR 2 8 1992 RET'D			

BOWLING GREEN STATE UNIVERSITY LIBRARY DISCARDED

DEMCO 38-297

HN800.N5B35
Barrett, Stanley R
Two villages on stilts;
economic and family change
in Nigeria

A113   0355051 8